Einstein &
the Art *of*
Mindful Cycling

$$E = {}_m c^2$$

Einstein &
the Art *of*
Mindful Cycling

Achieving Balance in the Modern World

Ben Irvine

METRO BOOKS
NEW YORK

For Rebecca

METRO BOOKS
New York

An Imprint of Sterling Publishing
387 Park Avenue South
New York, NY 10016

METRO BOOKS and the distinctive Metro Books logo are trademarks of
Sterling Publishing Co., Inc.

Text copyright © Ben Irvine 2012
Design and layout copyright © Ivy Press Limited 2012

This book was conceived, designed, and produced by

Leaping Hare Press
210 High Street, Lewes
East Sussex BN7 2NS, UK

Creative Director PETER BRIDGEWATER
Publisher SUSAN KELLY
Commissioning Editor MONICA PERDONI
Art Director WAYNE BLADES
Senior Editor JAYNE ANSELL
Designer GINNY ZEAL
Illustrator SARAH YOUNG

ISBN 978-1-4351-5673-9

For information about custom editions, special sales, and premium and
corporate purchases, please contact Sterling Special Sales at 800-805-5489 or
specialsales@sterlingpublishing.com.

Manufactured in China

Color origination by Ivy Press Reprographics

2 4 6 8 10 9 7 5 3 1

www.sterlingpublishing.com
www.leapingharepress.co.uk

CONTENTS

Acknowledgments

◆

Above all, a huge thank you to Rebecca Watts. Her advice, attention to detail, creativity, and all-round support made this book so much better and writing it so much more enjoyable.

Thanks also to Mark Powell and Daniel James Paterson, who read my drafts and advised on technical matters relating to cycling and Einstein's work.

This book wouldn't have been possible without *Cycle Lifestyle*, a project that has involved numerous contributors; I am grateful to them all, especially Dominic Tyerman, Gareth Jenkins, Adam Copeland, Jon Haste, David Amos and Morris Lautman at Barclays Print, Matt Dettmar, Rose Stowell, Richard Lawson, and Stuart France.

I am also grateful to the publishing team at Ivy Press for giving me this opportunity and being so personable and helpful throughout, and to Mark Williamson for putting us in touch.

Finally, thanks to the authors Walter Isaacson, Robert Penn, Richard Layard, Jonty Heaversedge, and Ed Halliwell for writing the books that, more than most, inspired mine.

$$E = {}_m c^2$$

A BALANCED MIND

If I tell you that riding a bicycle can make
you think like Albert Einstein, you probably
won't believe me. Einstein was one of history's greatest
scientists. Riding a bike is as easy as—well, riding a
bike. What if I remind you of the famous photograph
of Einstein cheerfully pedaling along? You might
wonder whether wearing pants that are too short
or a buttoned-up cardigan can make you any
more like this enigmatic genius
than cycling ever could.

THINK LIKE EINSTEIN

◆

Great thinkers are often as mysterious to us as the mysteries their pioneering work helped explain. Einstein was no different. His life was full of eccentricities, surprises, and contrasts, and at first it's not obvious we can learn much from them.

EINSTEIN WAS A REBEL (or a "lazy dog," as one of his college professors put it), and took nine years to get an academic job after graduating—yet in one legendary "miracle year," while working as a patent clerk in 1905, he published four astonishing papers that revolutionized physics. He was a committed believer in truth and the mathematical structure of reality—yet he declared that "imagination is more important than knowledge," and loved to play the violin. He valued simple, homely pleasures, preferring to help local children with their homework over adopting the gaudy trappings of his success—yet he became a global celebrity, a self-styled world citizen, and an impassioned advocate of international government. He was a scatterbrain who often forgot to wear socks and eat lunch—yet he campaigned unflaggingly for democracy, racial equality, and pacifism.

◆

I thought of that while riding my bicycle.

ALBERT EINSTEIN (1879–1955), ON HIS THEORY OF RELATIVITY

◆

A socialist who championed freedom, a loner who cared deeply for humanity, a nonbeliever who saw the universe as God's handiwork—Einstein was *Time* magazine's "person of the century," yet also the inspiration behind E. T. and Yoda. On his deathbed he was still scrawling equations.

Unity in Difference

The wonderful world of Einstein contains all this, and more. What a jumbled-up genius! Or so it can seem; but one man's jumble is another man's blend. Just as Einstein's theories spied unity in the diversity of nature, his own life was more coherent than a first glance suggests. The local and the global, the individual and the social, the creative and the practical— in Einstein's world each was perfectly harmonized. None was sacrificed for the others. His worldview was balanced. And that's why Einstein and cycling belong together.

The View from the Bike

This book is about how cycling can help us all achieve the same mindful balance that Einstein managed—among local, global, individual, social, creative, and practical ways of living. In the modern world, it often seems as though we have to choose between each of these, but on a bicycle we don't, because cycling threads them all together into a glorious feeling of well-being. Local sensibilities meet broad horizons, expansive freedoms meet friendly communities, buzzing imaginations meet useful skills. Just as Einstein scaled intellectual peaks and saw previously unseen and wonderful patterns, the humble bicycle can help us rise above our hectic lives, shaping our views of the world and of one another for the better.

WHAT IS MINDFULNESS?

◆

"There are two ways to live life," Einstein once remarked: "as though nothing is a miracle, and as though everything is." Living mindfully is like experiencing everything as a miracle. If you're curious about what that means, then in a way you already know.

IN EXPERIENCING EVERYTHING AS A MIRACLE, Einstein didn't go around constantly proclaiming "It's a miracle" and dropping to his knees. He was simply in a state of *wonder*—being *curious*. He was keeping *aware* of things around him, paying *attention* to what he saw, and *observing* little details. Instead of cruising through life on autopilot, or ignoring the world as though it were a car alarm unnoticed in the background, Einstein remained alive to his surroundings and the amazing secrets they might reveal. He lived as if constantly enthralled by the flickering flames of a fire.

◆

I have no special talents. I am only passionately curious.

EINSTEIN

◆

Mindfulness as Meditation

Meditation isn't just for hippies trying to connect with another dimension. Usually people practice meditation— whether Buddhists or businesspeople—for the thoroughly down-to-earth reason that mindfulness is a practical skill we can improve in, with benefits proven by science. It's like exercising. Just as we can build up our muscles by going to the gym, we can become more mindful by meditating, actually altering our brains in the process. Through disciplining our curiosity, we can learn to focus better.

◆

We might discover a lot more about ourselves and the world around us if we were able to pay more attention to the present moment, right here and now.

FROM "THE MINDFUL MANIFESTO"
DR. JONTY HEAVERSEDGE & ED HALLIWELL, HAY HOUSE, 2010

◆

Going with the Flow

Although the goal of mindfulness is to approach *everything* curiously, meditation usually begins with being curious about ourselves. This isn't because meditators are self-obsessed— quite the opposite. Meditation, like charity, begins "at home," because this is where we get distracted most easily. We get caught up in our thoughts, sensations, and feelings, either trying to suppress or vent them or worrying about their origins and consequences. Being mindful of ourselves in meditation helps us avoid these struggles. Instead of *judging* our thoughts, sensations, and feelings, we become curious about them. We simply *witness* them passing through the present moment like clouds in natural formations. In using one part of our minds to calmly observe another, we allow the contents of our inner lives to find their own balance, and we become more curious about the world outside.

Sometimes when performing a task mindfully, we enter a state that psychologists call *flow*—also known as being "in the zone." We become so focused that we lose ourselves, that is, we forget about our own minds in whatever we are doing— whether playing sports or music, creating an artwork, knitting, gardening, or writing a book. Although mindfulness and flow are seemingly very different experiences, there is an intuitive connection between them. Our minds drift into flow whenever we're fully at peace with our thoughts, sensations, and feelings.

Creating Happiness

Being in flow is one of the greatest human pleasures. The more we experience flow, the happier our lives are. Maybe that's why Einstein, who had legendary powers of concentration, was so cheerful.

Most probably, though, his happiness was a cause as well as an effect of his prolific output. We commonly hear that geniuses are tortured souls, but surely this isn't entirely true.

MINDFUL BREATHING

✳

One of the aims of meditating is to learn how to *be*. This may sound peculiar, but that's because most of us are more familiar with *doing* than being. If we're not racing around busily, then our minds are. There's always something to worry about.

Beneath all this agitation, one part of us keeps a steadier pace—our breathing. We can use our breath as an anchor to remind us to stay in the present for a while. We don't need to worry about breathing. We do it automatically. It is the basis of our being, the gentle rhythm of our lives.

Find a quiet place and a firm surface to sit on. Try to sit as straight as possible, perhaps cross-legged on the floor, or upright on a chair. Keep your lips slightly apart, and just breathe naturally. As you begin to settle, notice the in-and-out rhythm of your breath. Don't try to control it. Let it be. Place your attention on the paths of your breath—through your nostrils, past your lips, into your throat, and in and out of your chest and abdomen. Observe all these sensations.

You'll find that your mind keeps getting distracted. That is normal. The aim of meditation is not to have an empty mind. Simply notice your thoughts and feelings as if they were raindrops on a windowpane. Instead of getting caught up in them or shielding yourself from them, just bring your attention gently back to your breathing. Over and over again, return to your breath, a base camp for your wandering mind.

Try this meditation for ten minutes, and you'll have experienced your first taste of mindfulness—some breathing space in a hectic modern world.

Even tragic figures, such as Vincent van Gogh, Friedrich Nietzsche, and Samuel Beckett, were able to stop agonizing long enough to get on with their prodigious labors—and, in general, the more contented we are, the more productive and creative we are. "Be regular and ordered in your life," advised Flaubert, "so you can be violent and original in your work."

Recent times have seen a lot of interest, including scientific research, into how we can live more happily, and various themes recur. Happiness, it seems, has multiple causes—including learning, giving, exercising, supportive families, caring communities, job satisfaction, financial stability, security, health, values, political freedom, flow ... and mindfulness.

Mindfully Happy

Being mindful is arguably the most important of these. For one thing, it helps us avoid being *un*happy. Through being aware of ourselves—the way we think, the way we act, the way we react—we can avoid getting caught in the negative patterns of behavior that are characteristic of anxiety, depression, or addiction. We can learn to let unwanted impulses go, and relax.

Mindfulness also promotes the other causes of happiness. Sometimes the connections are specific. For instance, being mindful strengthens our immune systems, and it has been proven to have a positive effect on illnesses, such as AIDS and cancer, as well as psychosomatic conditions and chronic pain.

Being mindful helps us to learn by making us curious. It helps keeps our finances stable by costing nothing and by encouraging conscientiousness in all areas of our lives.

This example hints at the most general connection between mindfulness and happiness. In learning to be mindful, we become better at understanding ourselves, noticing how our behavior makes us feel, and being aware enough to make changes. We nurture ourselves, becoming our own mentor, and choose to fill our lives with things that bring us happiness.

Mindful Compassion

If this still sounds a little self-obsessed, then don't worry—many of the causes of happiness are sociable. The most obvious example is *giving*—being kind, helpful, or generous toward others. Giving will more probably make us happy than selfishness will, as counterintuitive as that may sound. The same goes for having moral values, through which we aspire to give others the treatment we would want to receive ourselves.

Mindfulness, too, is sociable. At the least, it helps us pay more attention to others; but, more than this, understanding ourselves helps us to understand others better, too, so we

◆

The value of a man resides in what he
gives and not in what he is capable of receiving.

EINSTEIN

◆

develop a heightened sense of empathy and compassion. We approach others in the same nonjudgmental way that we approach ourselves, which makes us less critical and defensive in our interactions. Mindful people tend to be better communicators, and they have relationships that are more satisfying and less troubled by conflict and stress.

Social Capital

When our families and communities are built from these kinds of mindful relationships, our lives are enriched with "social capital"—all those friendly and useful social engagements that occur within groups of people. Economists often think of social capital as a *resource*, equivalent to possessions or money, but that's only part of the story. What we notice most when we are lucky enough to have a lot of social capital in our lives is not the increased efficiency or profitability of our days, but the warm sense of belonging each day brings.

Modern Mindlessness

You may be thinking that it's easy to be mindful when you're sitting by a mountain stream, happy when you're enjoying good company, or compassionate when you're a nun, but it's not always so easy for those of us in the modern world. Being mindful is hard when we're bombarded with distractions. Advertisements provoke desires we didn't know we had. News reports shock us with catastrophes, crimes, and controversies. Bombastic celebrities make the calm seem dull. Our in-boxes fill up too fast for us to bail them out. Then, of course, there's the Internet: the ultimate distractor.

Being happy is hard when our lives are so stressful. Long working hours and grueling commutes make us unwell, and we still struggle to pay the bills. We're too tired to exercise, so we put on weight. We buy flashy clothes and possessions, but we still feel insecure, and there's no time left for us to learn or be creative, or even hang out with our families and friends. To relax, we reach for the bottle.

Being compassionate is hard when everyone else is so hardened. From corrupt bankers and politicians to criminals and welfare cheats, few seem to deserve our sympathy. Meanwhile, social capital can be hard to come by—we're all too busy watching TV, playing video games, and suing each other. Many of us don't even know our neighbors' names. Values seem like luxuries in tough economic times.

The World Needs Mindfulness

Much of modern life is mind*less*. But that's no reason to give up. As the American politician Charles W. Tobey once said, "The things that are wrong with the country today are the sum total of all the things that are wrong with us as individuals." This means that if we want to live in a more mindful, compassionate society, each of us must become a more mindful, compassionate person. The only question is how.

MINDFUL CYCLING

◆

Developing mindfulness is like developing any skill, such as playing a musical instrument, performing surgery, or flying a lunar module—the idea is to build and consolidate our capabilities in a controlled environment before applying our learning to real-life situations.

WHEN WE CULTIVATE A SENSE OF CURIOSITY in meditation, we are hoping the effects will apply throughout the day and beyond. Alas, the bedlam of modern life sometimes overwhelms us and dulls our senses. Even people who regularly meditate may find it hard to stay mindful all the time. Wouldn't it be great if we could actually *live* more meditatively—practicing as we go, on the hoof, with no distinction between the rehearsal and the performance?

This is where the bicycle comes in—a dream machine that blends meditation with movement; curiosity with velocity; freedom with fenders. On a bicycle, you can achieve in a few weeks an art that Buddhist monks spend decades learning, and which the great Einstein encapsulated effortlessly: *mindful living*. No wonder the bicycle is often called the best invention in history; it's a simple, easy-to-use device that can inspire us to wonderful psychological heights. Now that's what I call a miracle. This book will explain how it happens.

A dream machine that blends meditation with movement ...

The Reach of Cycling

There's only one thing wrong with bikes, and it's the one thing they have in common with *Dr. Who*'s Daleks—they can't go upstairs. So, alas, we can't be on bikes all the time. But we *can* ride to work and back, and to the stores, to the park, to see friends, to take the kids to school, or even to the ends of the earth. Thanks to all these bicycle journeys, the modern world is richer in mindfulness.

And that's not the limit of cycling's positive influence. Not only do bikes enable us to combine mindfulness with living, they have the same spillover effect as conventional meditation. In other words, cycling makes us feel mindful throughout the day, even after we've hopped off our bikes. Any cyclist will tell you how alert yet calm, and energized yet relaxed they feel after cycling, and how much easier it is to concentrate. They'll also tell you how much happier cycling makes them feel in general and better connected with their communities.

With all these benefits to share, devout cyclists can sometimes sound a little evangelical about their passion, and they may come across as annoying or even patronizing. But you can hardly blame them for their eagerness to let others in on the secret. Often the cynicism directed at cyclists says more about others' disillusionment, or even resentment—an exhilarated grin might look like a smirk if you're stuck in traffic.

Or maybe people get irked because not all cyclists are saintly. There are plenty of mindless ways to cycle—on the sidewalk, the wrong way up a one-way street, without lights at night, through a stop sign, drunk, distracted by an iPod, in a blustering hurry, talking on a cell phone, or with total ignorance of the rules of the road. When I talk about mindful cycling, I'm not talking about these inconsiderate cyclists.

Such people are, in a way, squandering an opportunity. Fostering mindfulness, I would say, is a bicycle's true calling —its métier. Consider, for instance, how a hammock is perfectly designed for dozing in, and how any other use of it is either nonoptimal (say, using it as a swing), or foolhardy (say, using it as a trampoline). Just as a bicycle can bring out the best in a person, mindful cycling brings out the best in a bike.

Achieving Balance

By helping us to avoid getting caught up in our thoughts, sensations, and feelings, cycling can bring our whole worldview into balance, whether as individuals or as a society. This whole is made up of four general "attitudes," which correspond to the four chapters here. Insofar as the book balances these attitudes, you could think of it as being infused with mindfulness.

In "The Greatest Invention," we encounter the "practical" attitude—a scientific or technological approach whereby we seek to understand, control, and predict reality. In "Freewheeling," we discover the "individual" attitude, whereby we seek to express ourselves freely, creatively, and determinedly. In "Around the Block," we find the "local" attitude, whereby we seek simplicity, modesty, and community. In "Around the World," we discern the "global" attitude, whereby we seek international integration and a sense of common humanity.

Each chapter begins by revealing aspects of Einstein's personality that exemplify one of these attitudes, and goes on to show how cycling can bring about a similar mindset. Einstein's life encapsulated mindfulness; together the four chapters of this book give some insight into his holistic philosophy, and illustrate how the humble bicycle can help us all to achieve a comparable balance.

The Four Attitudes

Every cyclist knows that leaning too far in any direction upsets a natural balance. Using the human brain as a metaphor, we can think of each direction as representing one of the four attitudes. The left side of the brain specializes in understanding mechanisms, rules, and artificial systems—so we can think of the practical attitude as left leaning. The right side of the brain specializes in creativity, self-awareness, and imagination—so the individual attitude can be considered as right leaning. At the back of the brain are areas specializing in basic emotions and needs—so we can construe the local attitude as backward leaning. Finally, the distinctively human frontal regions of the brain enable us to see our lives in the context of a wider perspective—so the global attitude can be thought of as forward leaning.

On a bicycle we remain centered—we manage not to lean too far forward or backward, left or right—in more ways than one. This is the art of mindful cycling—and the key to achieving balance in the modern world.

HOW I LOST & REGAINED MY BALANCE

◆

When I was a teenager, I aspired to be a great thinker, a maverick—someone just like Einstein. I read avidly and kept a diary of theories, lyrics, and philosophical thoughts. They were juvenile musings, of course. But the great thing about getting your inspiration from historical figures is that you don't care what anyone else thinks.

I DIDN'T CARE, FOR INSTANCE, that cycling in those days was considered unfashionable. I figured that getting to college in ten minutes on a bike was better than spending half an hour on a bus, even if I had to put up with my brother calling me a geek. As it turns out, he's an eager cyclist these days (a fact I never tire of pointing out to him). But I suppose he was right about me being a geek. I ended up going to university, where I lived up to my epithet and completed a PhD in philosophy.

Losing My Way

But throughout my education—I don't know why—I gradually lost my balance. It wasn't just that I stopped cycling (but it's true, I did). It was that my life stopped going smoothly.

The standard things went wrong: my friendships, romances, family, health, career, and lifestyle. While these problems were racking up, I wasn't helped by my chosen vocation. Most philosophizing involves seeking out life's dilemmas, paradoxes, and puzzles; never accepting situations with all their conflicts and absurdities. I used to veer between extremes, either pushing too far in one direction, or pushing something important away in another. Even my ambition became a curse. I was focusing on the achievements of other people, such as Einstein, but not on what I could learn from their journeys. I was never in the moment; never relaxed; never comfortable with the status quo; never really happy.

The Turning Point

And then I hit rock bottom. It was five o'clock in the morning, in December 2009, when I woke up, face down, on the sidewalk somewhere in London, my head spinning, tears in my eyes, alone. I didn't know what had happened, except that I'd been drinking. Cars were revving past, strangers were stepping over me. I had no money and there was no one I could call. The wheels had well and truly come off my life.

It was not long after this that I took up cycling again. I'm not really sure why, but I started making the same kinds of local cycle trips I'd made as a boy—to the stores, friends' houses, out and about in the evenings—and soon I was riding for the hell of it, exploring a side of London unknown to me even when I was growing up: peaceful canals, gorgeous city parks, intriguing backstreets, and secret alleys.

So much beauty and possibility! And for so long it had been hiding behind a facade of shouty main streets and grimy window-panes—that distracting veneer of familiarity which you never think to question.

◆

When the spirits are low, when
the day appears dark, when work becomes
monotonous, when hope hardly seems worth having,
just mount a bicycle and go out for a spin down the
road, without thought on anything but the
ride you are taking.

SIR ARTHUR CONAN DOYLE (1859–1930)

◆

Feeling Better

I was soon experiencing something different in myself: a nostalgic feeling that I can only describe as *joy*. Sometimes it would happen halfway down a freewheeling descent, or, with a touch of *Schadenfreude*, as I wove my way through a traffic jam, past grumpy-looking car drivers.

Other times it would happen for no obvious reason; maybe it was the wind ruffling the back of my hair; the glittering cityscape dancing from side to side in my vision like a grinning gospel choir; or a few friendly words exchanged with a fellow cyclist at the lights. I soon realized that this nostalgic feeling was also becoming a hopeful one. I began to look to the future from a place of happiness.

And so it was that I changed as a person, and gradually repaired the things that had gone wrong in my past. I'm not saying that cycling was the solution to all my problems; it's just that being on a bike gave me a break from the rest of my life, a quiet place to draw inspiration from. Cycling helped me to think up solutions, and I soon found myself making constructive decisions off the bike, too. It's funny how these things snowball. That joyful cyclist cruising equably through the wilderness of life became the real me.

Moving On

I'm telling you this because it's a journey anyone can make. The global economy hit rock bottom at around the same time I did. It seems that the whole damn system is a mess—with governments, the media, businesses, and banks in collusion, and everyone pointing the finger at everyone else.

Amid the bedlam of claim and counterclaim, it can be hard to imagine a way out. But some people have made it, just like Einstein did in his life, slipping quietly away from familiar distractions and into those forgotten byways where well-being dwells and the chaos of modern life is balanced and becalmed.

If you haven't made it yet, then this book is about how to cycle there. It's easier than you might think. *You never forget how to ride a bike.*

CHAPTER ONE

$$E = _m c^{2}$$

THE GREATEST INVENTION

Cycling equips us with a "practical"
attitude, just like Einstein's. By reflecting on
the ingenious design of the bicycle and how it came to
be that way, we appreciate the importance of invention.
In learning how to maintain a bike, we develop an
understanding of how things work, and of the joy
of working with material things. We become more
enterprising in our activities, more scientific in our
outlook, and better prepared in our lives.
We are mindful of reality.

METHOD IN THE MADNESS

◆

Despite being midsummer in the coastal resort of Watch Hill, Rhode Island, it had started to rain heavily. Einstein, who had been enjoying his vacation, was taking a ride in the passenger seat of an open-top convertible. Undaunted, he reached for his hat—but not in the way you might expect. Einstein reached toward his head, only to remove his hat and place it in his coat pocket, much to the confusion of driver Peter Bucky, who eyed him quizzically. "My hair has withstood water many times before," explained Einstein, "but I don't know how many times my hat can."

THIS KIND OF BEHAVIOR FUELS the popular image of Einstein; that inscrutably eccentric genius with whirling white hair. Yet there's more to the story—and Einstein—than meets the eye. In a way, his decision wasn't so strange. The downpour might have caused his beloved hat to become frayed and misshapen; his hair already was. Einstein, believe it or not, showed good practical awareness.

When you think about it, how could it be otherwise for a great scientist? As someone who devoted his life to understanding the subtleties of the universe, much of Einstein's behavior was probably based on factors beyond normal consideration. And even when, undoubtedly, he was absent-minded—whether locking himself out of his house on his wedding night, or clapping at the announcement of his own

name at an awards ceremony because he was deep in thought—
Einstein's preoccupations were probably the worldlier. He
may have seemed unearthly, but he was fluent in reality.

A Life of Invention

When we praise someone's invention, we usually mean a particular device they've created, or the process of creating it.
But when we say someone has led "a life of invention," we are
using the word to compliment a whole person—someone
with a *general* talent for understanding, and working with,
material things. We could certainly say this about Einstein.

Invention was in his nature and nurture. Shortly after his
birth in 1879 in Ulm, Germany, Einstein's family relocated to
Munich, where his father, Hermann, and his Uncle Jakob set
up a company manufacturing and installing electrical equip-
ment. By 1885, they commanded a workforce of 200 people
and provided the city's Oktoberfest with its first electric
lights. Jakob received six patents in engineering.

The young Einstein was soon showing similar aptitude.
He delighted in building fourteen-story houses of cards, and
after his father gave him a navigational compass, Einstein
would fixate on the needle, wondering what was making it
move. When his mother, Pauline, gave birth to his sister
Maria, Einstein responded with that arresting inquisitiveness
that would one day become his trademark: "Yes," he said,
looking at the baby, "but where are the wheels?"

Throughout his education, the theme continued. Excelling in mathematics and physics, Einstein's enquiries always seemed to go beyond the pale. His teachers found his irreverent curiosity exasperating—not least when he caused an explosion in the lab.

◆

Everything should be made as
simple as possible, but not simpler.

EINSTEIN

◆

The Worldly Cloister

With a good eye for an invention, but lukewarm academic references, it was no surprise that Einstein ended up working as a patent examiner instead of an assistant professor. As "Technical Expert Third Class," his role was to judge the merits of each application received. The job hardly seemed ideal, but Einstein would one day look back favorably upon that "worldly cloister where I hatched my most beautiful ideas." His boss benevolently turned a blind eye to him working on physics papers during office hours, and assessing others' ideas helped Einstein acquire valuable scientific habits: a critical spirit, an appreciation of simplicity, and an ability to imagine how hypotheses would pan out in reality.

And so it was that this outsider stunned the world of physics with a series of elegant but powerful new theories, including relativity, the wave-particle duality of light, and the equation $E=mc^2$. Although these ideas remain difficult for laypeople to understand, Einstein always endeavored to anchor his mathematics in reality through vivid analogies: a painter falling off a house, an elevator accelerating through empty space, or a bicycle riding alongside a light beam.

Einstein's Realism

Einstein believed that the world exists, and that we should seek to understand how it works. Strangely, some people disagree with him. Many philosophers claim that the world doesn't exist, only opinions do—that if one man thinks the Eiffel Tower is in Paris and another thinks it is in London, both are right. This is equivalent to saying that science is pointless; we might as well just make things up.

This viewpoint is often called "relativism," because reality is said to be "relative" to a person's opinions. Einstein was irritated when people confused relativity with relativism. When, in 1919, the astronomer Arthur Eddington produced photographic evidence that proved Einstein's theory to be true, opinions didn't come into it.

◆

Truth hurts. Maybe not as much as jumping on
a bicycle with the seat missing, but it hurts.

LIEUTENANT FRANK DREBIN
IN "THE NAKED GUN 2½," 1991

◆

Einstein was also perturbed when some of his colleagues drew a peculiar conclusion from his work. Their "uncertainty principle" held that physicists' observations can influence the way the world is. Einstein spent the last forty years of his life opposing this suggestion. "Belief in an external world independent of the perceiving subject is the basis of all natural science," he insisted.

Einstein's insistence was considered stubborn, which is a familiar criticism of scientists. But it is hardly fair to criticize science for a lack of humility. Science responds to its doubts by trying to discover more about the world. This is exactly why Einstein's impressive work gained credibility.

To say that the world doesn't exist and that all opinions are equally valid seems lazy in comparison. Some people become relativists because they can't face the truth; others are just being insincere. When speaking about his contrary colleagues, Einstein advised: "Don't listen to their words, fix your attention on their deeds." What he was getting at is that people tend to take the world more seriously when it comes to actually *doing* things. If someone ever tells you the world doesn't exist, invite them to jump out of a fourteen-story window.

Einstein's Century

Einstein occasionally helped out with his father's engineering business. He also dabbled in inventing, coming up with a noiseless refrigerator, a machine for measuring low-voltage electricity, and toys made out of matchboxes and string for his children. Yet Einstein never became a professional inventor. He disliked working with "a bleak capital gain as the goal."

And he had seen technology's downsides, in two world wars. Even his own theories were used by the American government to unleash nuclear weapons on Japan in 1945. Science, Einstein warned, had given people "the means to poison and mutilate one another," while in peacetime it had "made our lives hurried and uncertain" and "enslaved men to machines," making them work "long wearisome hours mostly without joy in their labor." Instead, Einstein implored, the goal of science should always be to make life better for ordinary people: "Never forget this when you are pondering over your diagrams and equations."

Einstein's influence on science in the twentieth century is incomparable. In physics his breakthroughs led to the discovery of dark stars, black holes, antimatter, and wormholes. The rebellious young Einstein would have loved the wacky universe his theories helped uncover. But it is in technology where this reluctant inventor has been most influential. Billions of ordinary people have undoubtedly benefited from advancements made possible thanks to Einstein's dedication to discovery. These include lasers, cement mixing, aerosols, nuclear power, fiber optics, semiconductors, satellites, solar panels, computers, dairy production, and many more. But where are the wheels?

THE PEOPLE'S NAG

◆

Horses love cycling. Not because they love to cycle, but because bicycles allowed horses to put their hooves up and relax after 5,000 years of loyal service to humanity. The only question still bothering horses (and historians) is why it took so long for the bicycle to be invented, despite the technology being simple and available for millennia.

THE WHEEL WAS INVENTED at roughly the same time as horses were first domesticated—too far back in time to be sure who was the first to accomplish either. Originating in southern Mesopotamia, the earliest known wheels were wooden dishes with a hole in the middle for the axle of a carriage to pass through. It wasn't until 500 BCE that the Egyptians began crafting wheels with spokes to make their chariots lighter and faster. Wheel technology then remained pretty much unchanged until the beginning of the nineteenth century.

At this time—in an era of great technological progress—an amazing, century-long quest was underway: to create a human-powered land vehicle, the so-called "people's nag." Some of the earliest efforts relied on sails (which were unreliable and unwieldy) or even slaves (which was cheating). In 1819, one British journalist surveyed the scene and declared that "the completion of a machine or carriage for traveling, without horses or animals to drag it" would be "the proudest triumph of mechanics."

The Running Machine

Fittingly, the invention of cycling was a journey—a relay, you might say, in which the bicycle as we know it today emerged by stages in the hands of numerous separate innovators. When I'm riding along, I often imagine all those pioneering bicycle inventors going about their business, trying to make the world better in some small way. The bicycle's gradual development reminds me that nothing great comes without sweat; that excellence never falls to earth fully formed. Cycling's collaborative history reminds me that invention is boosted by teamwork; that one person's ideas can amplify another's. The haphazard nature of the journey reminds me that hard work sometimes pays off in strange ways; you never know what wonderful surprises may be waiting around the corner.

◆

I was standing on the shoulders of giants.

EINSTEIN, ON HIS PREDECESSORS

◆

The Draisine

The man who kick-started the development of the bicycle was an eccentric German baron called Karl von Drais. In 1815, a volcano had erupted in Indonesia, killing around 90,000 people and covering Europe in a huge ash cloud that shut out the sun. Harvests failed, and farmers were forced to shoot their starving horses. Drais resolved to discover that elusive people's nag.

The "Draisine" was essentially a bicycle without pedals or brakes, with a pole attached to the front wheel for steering. Apart from the iron strips on its wheels, the whole contraption was made of wood. Drais unveiled his invention in 1817, calling it a "running machine." The rider had to push off the ground, one foot after the other, as though running, and between steps the momentum carried the vehicle along. When coasting downhill, no legwork was needed—a perk that Drais may have recognized as an unintended consequence, while lifting up his feet like an exuberant child. One way or another, he had discovered the principle of using propulsion to balance on two wheels.

Unfortunately, stopping the thing wasn't much fun. Riders frequently suffered ignominious dismounts (otherwise known as falling off), or rode into pedestrians. Despite flurries of manufacturing in cities across the United States and Europe, the running machine was invariably banned from sidewalks, and most people scornfully dismissed it as a "dandy horse." Soon, even dedicated riders became disillusioned with its inefficiency and its tendency to wear out shoes. The development of the bicycle fell into obscurity for fifty years.

The Boneshaker

During this period, most engineers focused their efforts on four-wheeled contraptions, with little success. Some designs featured wings that were supposed to flap as the operator

MINDFULNESS OF MECHANISMS

❋

We rarely take time to appreciate the many clever mechanisms that make modern life so convenient. Some represent thousands of years of progress, yet we typically use mechanical devices mindlessly, without giving a thought to the ingenuity that went into creating them.

Next time you encounter a working bicycle, take a moment to admire its mechanical brilliance. Notice the chain. See how its alternating series of bushings and pins connect to make a flexible but strong spine, which embraces sets of toothy sprockets on the pedal shaft and rear wheel. See how the pedals spin on their own axes while the cranks turn, just as the moon spins while the earth rotates around the sun.

Lift the handlebars slightly to raise the front wheel off the ground. Turn the wheel, observing the circle it traces in the air. Notice the whirring spokes, and imagine how cleverly they enable the whole wheel to deform as it hits the ground before returning to its original shape, as a squashed tennis ball will.

Turn the handlebars, seeing how the front fork is slid through the tubular frame, combining rigidity with suppleness. See the brakes waiting patiently until they're called for, to yank a cable that drags rectangles of rubber onto the rims of the wheel, halting the bicycle as if time were slowing down.

Notice the diamond-shape frame, expertly welded at its joints. It is hollow, mostly air, yet will hold itself and all the bike's components together through decades of miles.

Be curious about a bicycle, and it will transport your mind as well as your body.

worked the drive on the rear wheels; others required three men to pull levers; one carriage moved by treadles shifting back and forth, as on a sewing machine; there was even a Draisine-style kick-propulsion vehicle with four wheels.

Inventors, it seems, distrusted the idea of balancing on two wheels—the same prejudice, perhaps, that had delayed the invention of the bicycle by thousands of years. Some commentators even became skeptical about the prospect of *any* viable human-powered vehicle. In 1832 the editor of *Mechanics Magazine* declared that "man is a locomotive machine of Nature's own making, not to be improved by the addition of any cranks or wheels."

The Breakthrough

He was wrong. Two cranks and two wheels wrong. A few decades later, the two-wheeler made a stunning comeback, with the simple addition of pedal-operated cranks attached to the front wheel. By pushing down alternately on the pedals to rotate the cranks, the rider could achieve at all times the balanced forward propulsion that on the running machine had only been possible when coasting downhill.

When a flock of birds alters its course, it can be difficult to determine which individual changed direction first. Likewise, it is hard to establish exactly *who* was responsible for the breakthrough that turned the running machine into a cycling machine—there were so many innovators in the picture.

Pierre Michaux began manufacturing pedal bicycles in his shop in Paris in 1867 and would later claim priority for the invention; but his business partners, the brothers Aimé and René Olivier, and Georges de la Bouglise, almost certainly did more of the inventive work. Another Parisian, Pierre Lallement, also claimed credit, and, indeed, patented a similar design in the United States in 1866. Further complicating the story were posthumous claims that, independently of one another, Scotsmen Gavin Dalzell and Kirkpatrick Macmillan had, decades earlier, privately engineered a novel form of bicycle featuring pedals connected to its rear wheel by rods.

What *is* certain is that the pedal bicycle first caught on in Paris in the late 1860s, and within just a few years could be seen on every continent, in cities and beyond. The machine became known as the "boneshaker" on account of the rough experience its wooden wheels and iron frame gave riders. But unlike the running machine, the boneshaker began evolving immediately. New firms cropped up to meet demand, adding springs, spoked iron wheels, and solid rubber tires, to soften the ride. Other innovations included brakes and tubular frames. Novel efforts were also made to promote cycling, such as free lessons, indoor cycling rinks, exhibitions, clubs, and races, all of which helped to win over skeptics.

*There were so many
innovators in the picture.*

Room for Improvement

Yet the best bicycles of the day remained flawed. The biggest problem was that whenever the front wheel turned to the left or right, the pedals did the same, and the rider's legs were forced to follow. This caused the wheel to rub on the inside of the rider's thigh, or even drag the other leg into the spokes. Many doctors warned of the risks—particularly to men's tenderest parts. The machines, too, incurred damage easily, and performed badly on uneven surfaces. Forced onto smoother sidewalks, riders were still berated by stone-throwing pedestrians who saw the boneshaker—like the running machine—as a dangerous toy for the idle rich. And cycling was about to become even more hazardous and exclusive.

The High Wheeler

When it comes to old-fashioned bicycles, the most famous example is surely the high wheeler. This striking contraption had a huge front wheel and a smaller rear one, and was nicknamed the "Penny Farthing"—a reference to the size difference between two British coins that were in circulation at the time. Most people today wonder how such a ludicrous-looking vehicle could ever have been considered practical. Yet high wheelers were the racing cycles of their day, sporting the most cutting-edge cycle technology (such as rubber pedals, ball bearings, and lighter frames), and were also the first vehicles to earn the modern name "bicycle."

High wheelers emerged in Great Britain in the mid-1870s, and within a decade were available around the world. They gave riders an advantage for a simple reason. When pedals were attached to the center of a bicycle's front wheel, the bigger the wheel, the farther the rider traveled with each revolution of the pedals. Front wheels soon grew, up to a whopping 5 feet in diameter—their size limited only by whether riders' legs could reach the center.

The seat on a high wheeler was directly above the front wheel, since a downward force on the pedals was most powerful. Some models had a step built into the frame for getting up or down on. Both had to be done at a trot or the bicycle would topple. When up on the high wheeler, riders were obviously in a rather perilous position—the equivalent of sitting on the shoulders of a person sprinting. Falling off was known as a "header"—a dangerous experience made inevitable by bumpy roads, crosswinds, and the awkwardness of mounting and dismounting. These speedier, riskier machines tended to attract a certain kind of rider—fit, young, daredevil, usually (but not always) male. As one amateur opined, most people were "averse to mounting a thing like a giraffe."

If only something could be done to make cycling more accessible. One enthusiast speculated that "any invention that would enable the rider to stop altogether and still sit on the machine would do more to popularize bicycling than anything which has yet been done."

The Safety Bicycle

In a chorus of eurekas, the solution was discovered multiple times in the early 1880s. The brands may have been different—the Bicyclette, the Marvel, the Pioneer, the Antelope, the BSA, and the Humber—but each was an early example of a "safety" bicycle, the distinguishing feature of which was a chain connecting the pedals to the rear wheel.

Two things made these models safer. The first was gearing: the cog powered by the pedals was larger than the cog on the rear wheel, so the chain turned the rear wheel faster than the pedals rotated. It was now unnecessary for bicycles to feature a huge wheel to maximize pedal output, so the rider's sitting position could be lower. This made falls less severe and less likely, because the rider's feet could touch the ground, making it easier to mount and dismount, start and stop, and go slowly.

The second innovation was the transference of pedal power to the back wheel. This made the machine less prone to slide around, and freed up the front wheel to undertake its principal responsibility: steering.

The Rover Safety

The only residual problem with the earliest safety models was that they came in odd shapes, some with small front wheels or complicated frames. Despite the lower riding position making riders more aerodynamic and therefore faster, rickety rides were common.

Further innovations changed this. In 1886 John Kemp Star-
ley perfected his Rover Safety model. It featured wheels of
approximately equal size, a rigid diamond-shape frame with
an adjustable seat and handlebars, and the safety's characteristic rear wheel chain drive. Three years later, John Dunlop
invented the pneumatic tire, with an inner tube filled with
compressed air. All these improvements made for the safest,
lightest, quickest, and smoothest bicycles ever created, and
the essential form of the two-wheeler remains unchanged
today. The future had arrived, and the public went wild for it.

Cycling's Century

With the dream of a people's nag finally a reality, the early
1890s saw a worldwide explosion in cycling. Some claimed
falsely it was a fad; others predicted that cycling would continue "so long as men and women have legs," as one editor
put it. He hasn't been proven wrong yet. If Einstein was the
person of the twentieth century, then the bicycle, the most
popular personal transport ever, was undoubtedly the
machine of the century. Today, there are more than a billion
bicycles in the world, used for practical, recreational, and
sporting reasons, by young and old, rich and poor.

Cycling peaked during the economic depressions of the
first and fourth decades of the twentieth century, as well
as during the two world wars and the energy crisis of the
1970s. Throughout these ups and downs, a steady stream of

innovations improved the bicycle. The freewheel, which enables riders to rest their feet on the pedals while the back wheel rotates, became common, as did multiple gears and clever mechanisms, such as the elegant derailleur, for shifting between speeds. Calliper brakes were attached to handlebars, and the braking force was applied via pads or hydraulic disks. Detachable tires made it easier to repair punctures; vulcanization made the rubber stronger. New frame materials were used, such as aluminum, titanium, and carbon fiber, as well as durable enamel finishes and lightweight plastic components. Useful accessories emerged, including baskets, panniers, electric lights, and helmets. Next time you're on your bike, take a moment to contemplate all these inventions within an invention, and reflect on how many people have made a contribution to your pleasant cycle ride.

There have also been variations in the bicycle's form: for example, folding bikes (which can be packed away easily), mountain bikes (with shock absorbers and thick tires, for off-road cycling), and electric bikes (with batteries to assist with pedaling, or to power a throttle). Recumbent bikes have placed the rider even closer to the ground, enabling greater aerodynamic efficiency and record speeds in excess of 80 mph.

Pioneering Technology

Cycling also influenced other forms of material progress in the twentieth century. For instance, many technologies

---

It is curious that with the advent of the
automobile and the airplane, the bicycle is still
with us. Perhaps people like the world they can see from a
bike, or the air they breathe when they're out on a bike. Or
they like the bicycle's simplicity and the precision with which
it is made. Or because they like the feeling of being able to
hurtle through air one minute, and saunter through a park the
next, without leaving behind clouds of choking exhaust,
without leaving behind so much as a footstep.

GURDON S. LEETE, IN "THE QUOTABLE CYCLIST"
BREAKAWAY BOOKS, 2001

---

pioneered in bicycles, or in their manufacture and assembly, were subsequently employed in the development of automobiles and aviation. Indeed, some trailblazing automobile makers, including Henry Ford, were skilled bicycle mechanics, as were the Wright brothers, who invented the first airplane from out of their bicycle workshop.

As cycling grew in popularity, repair shops sprang up all over the world, which were then adapted into gas stations when the automobile became established. In addition, the widespread highway improvements that cyclists campaigned for literally paved the way for motorized transport. By inspiring greater mobility, both personal and automatic, cycling has been a vital lubricant in the emergence of the modern world.

A MATERIAL WORLD

◆

*"We are living in a material world, and I am a material girl," sang
Madonna in 1984. She wasn't the first—and won't be the last—to
question whether technological progress is really such a blessing.
People still wonder whether we have become too "materialistic" as a
culture; whether our interest in material things has become excessive.*

B UT MATERIALISM IS SURELY NOT THE RIGHT WORD for our
modern attitude. For one thing, unless we work as scientists, we don't generally understand how our possessions
work, so we pay little attention to them as material things.
With laptops, washing machines, and even toothbrushes
deploying space-age technology these days, most objects
bewilder rather than interest us.

Then there's our narcissistic attitude toward many modern
products. Like the vain youth Narcissus in the Greek myth,
who became obsessed with his own reflection on the surface
of a lake, we often fixate on what objects say about us, rather
than seeing them on their own terms. We want the coolest
gad-gets, the most fashionable clothes, or the most luxurious
furnishings, not because we're interested in these as material
things, but because we think they make us look good.

Finally, modern life often *screens* us from the world. Many
products create an artificial barrier distancing us from what is
happening in our surroundings. Virtual reality is an extreme

example of this, plying us with fake experiences through video games, social networking Web sites, or television programs. But there are other, less obvious, kinds of screening: for instance, earphones that block out the natural ambience; shrink-wrapped foods that bear no relation to their origins; or creditors who promise to lend us out of a situation that really calls for a dose of realism.

Immaterial World

Far from being interested in material things, many of us are bewildered by them, narcissistic about them, or screened from them. A better word for this attitude would be *imm*materialism—a *lack* of materialism. The more technology has advanced, which is a good thing, the more immaterialism has advanced too, which is a bad thing.

This correlation can explain Einstein's reservations about technological progress. We become enslaved to machines whenever we depend on them but do not understand them, once they have screened us from reality and made us inept. Our lives become hurried and uncertain whenever we forget to pause and be curious about the world. We work long and wearisome hours whenever we spend more money than we need to, on inessential products that we only want because we think they will make us look cool. We work without joy in our labor whenever we forsake the pleasures of endeavor for the mirages of one-upmanship.

Cycling brings us in tune with reality.

Immaterialism often causes negativity toward cycling. This is because the bicycle is unappealing to people who are ignorant about practical matters, who are afraid of being unconventional, and who prefer the comfort of a sanitized world. This is true of many automobile drivers, especially those who are dictated to by a satnav attached to the windshield of a flashy car they've never looked under the hood of. To such people, cyclists seem quaint, even stuck in the past.

But when the traffic stops, the engine fails, or the oil runs out, the resourceful cyclist will eventually speed by and show who's stuck in the present. The common caricatures get it back to front. Materialism is a virtue, and it's possessed by cyclists more than most. Both physically and mentally, cycling brings us in tune with reality.

Perfect Fit

Contrary to what greetings cards suggest, frogs can't cycle. Nor can cats. Monkeys can, surprisingly well. But humans do it best. However, before you get too triumphant about yet another thing you're better at than a monkey, keep in mind that the reason for your prowess is that human beings and bicycles are a perfect fit.

"The bicycle is a curious vehicle," said the Olympic cyclist John Howard: "Its passenger is its engine." This fact may be

curious when you think about it, but when you cycle it feels
completely natural to be part of the machinery. Sometimes as
I go along, I take the time to really notice the connection
between my body and my bike. I feel my hands gripping the
handlebars, strongly but effortlessly. I feel my buttocks on the
seat; I'm perched as though on a high wall, but totally stable,
as though floating on water. But most of all I feel the soft contact of my feet on the pedals; I sense my legs straightening and
bending alternately, so smoothly and intuitively that it feels
as though I'm being pedaled by the bike.

The cyclist is a man half made of flesh
and half of steel that only our century of science
and iron could have spawned.

LOUIS BAUDRY DE SAUNIER (1865–1938)
HISTOIRE GÉNÉRALE DE LA VÉLOCIPÉDIE, 1891

Indeed, Howard might have added that, in the case of
human beings, the bicycle's engine is located specifically in
the most powerful part of our bodies—our legs, where
40 percent of our anatomy belongs. The bicycle is tailored to
our strengths; no wonder riding one feels so effortless.

Not only this, cycling maximizes our athletic capacities.
When pedaling, we push down for only 60 degrees of the full
360-degree rotation, matching the optimum ratio between
effort and rest for our muscles.

Five Times Farther

The best thing about bicycles, however, is that they also amplify our efforts, incredibly effectively. With the same expenditure as walking, cycling can carry us up to five times the distance. This has been demon-

Bicycles amplify our efforts, incredibly effectively.

strated by scientific studies that have calculated how efficiently cycling converts energy into forward motion, compared to various animals. A human without a bicycle comes in at 34.2 calories per ounce per mile—which is respectable, albeit not as efficient as, say, horses or even salmon. With a bicycle, however, human energy efficiency increases fivefold, to about 6.8 calories per ounce per mile. No other animal achieves this figure. But the most astonishing thing is that no *machine* can either—including automobiles and airplanes. If bicycles ran on gasoline, they would travel nearly 3,100 miles per gallon.

◆

The bicycle is the perfect transducer to match
man's metabolic energy to the impedance of locomotion.
Equipped with this tool, man outstrips the efficiency of not only
all machines but all other animals as well.

IVAN ILLICH (1926–2002)
PHILOSOPHER

◆

Even when it comes to balancing, it seems that bicycles are eager to help us out. If you allow one to roll downhill on its own, it will automatically make tiny steering adjustments to remain upright. This is truly a machine that satisfies Einstein's insistence that technology should make life better for ordinary people.

Simple Cycles

Bicycles also satisfy Einstein's sense that inventors should keep things as simple as possible. Imagine you'd never heard of cycling, and someone told you about this amazing vehicle with so many advantages. You'd probably conjure up an image of a futuristic contraption, like something out of *Star Wars*. A couple of wheels attached to a diamond-shape set of tubes is something you'd think a bunch of preschoolers would come up with. I sometimes wonder what other wonderful inventions may be lurking undiscovered, too simple to have been considered.

The great thing about the simplicity of bicycles is that anyone can understand how they work, so anyone can develop the practical skills a regular cyclist needs. Through learning how (and when) to mend a puncture, replace or tighten brake pads, clean a chain or change a wheel, cyclists can gain proficiency in working with material things, a skill that fewer and fewer people seem to have these days. Even if a maintenance job is too tricky, at least cyclists can ask a real person at the repair shop to explain what needs to be done, and perhaps how to do it, in comprehensible terms. By encouraging greater practical awareness and facilitating hands-on experience, cycling can help us gain the confidence we need to approach some of the more complex and bewildering challenges of the modern world.

The bicycle was the last advance in technology everybody understands. Anybody who can ride one can understand how it works.

FROM "SPOKESONG" BY STEWART PARKER
STEWART PARKER: PLAYS 1, METHUEN DRAMA, 2000

In Praise of Preparedness

Another positive characteristic fostered by cycling is preparedness. Before setting off, riders need to plan a route and consider which accessories they'll need—hat, gloves, lights, helmet, spare clothes, waterproofs, and so on. This requires being organized and having foresight.

Sometimes being prepared involves optimization, which is familiar to any cyclist. It's an attitude of making the best of a situation—whether configuring your bike to be sure you get the most out of it (for instance, the optimal seat height is when your heels just touch the pedals with your legs straight), or configuring yourself to get the best out of cycling (having a healthy lifestyle and diet).

Effort & Reward

Cycling has long been associated with an enterprising spirit. The British phrase "get on your bike" is a cliché that cajoles would-be entrepreneurs, the unemployed, or the idle to look for work—yet the advice is essentially sound. With a set of wheels and little else, virtually anyone can make a success of themselves. Even the simple act of climbing a hill encourages staying power (as they say: "It's just a hill—get over it"), and enjoying the subsequent freewheeling descent reinforces an important association between effort and reward.

Other enterprising uses of bicycles are more quotidian. In urban settings, mail carriers, couriers, and even the emergency services get around on bikes. These kinds of hard-working people make the world go around.

A Bike is What it Does

Cyclists don't tend to be particularly worried about their image, so they don't usually get narcissistic about their bicycles. But the explanation also works in the other direction: there is something about cycling that discourages narcissism.

A bike "is what it does," Stewart Parker has said. This description is true of many products—sneakers, coffee makers, ironing boards. Anything designed to perform a particular task is what it does. But not all functioning products are *only* what they do. Consider sneakers. In the eyes of many people, your footwear symbolizes how fashionable you are.

When I was a kid in Great Britain, Dunlop sneakers meant you were a loser, Nike Air a winner. There wasn't much difference in the quality of these sneakers, but one was cheap, the other expensive. Today, more than ever, people are willing to pay more for socially impressive products.

Why aren't cyclists generally willing to pay premiums for trendy bikes? The reason, I think, is that there is such a huge difference in quality between various models. Depending on how well-engineered each is, it can be laborious or euphoric to ride, because factors such as speed, smoothness, and efficiency improve with quality (unfortunately, a lot of people give up cycling after one attempt, having ridden a clunker). The point is, if people are going to pay a lot for a bicycle, then how well it performs is usually their priority—narcissism doesn't come into it. (Granted, some people like to show off examples of good engineering; but, in this case, the product is the focus more than the owner.)

Knowing how to distinguish functions from fashions provides a crucial reality check against the wild and devious promises advertisers make to us day in, day out. Through cycling, we learn to consider: is the product offered really an improvement on what I already have? We also learn that paying premiums for a brand's image—from MP3 players and couches to chocolates and sneakers—can be a waste of our resources. In reminding us of these things, cycling steers us away from immaterialism.

Facing the World

A common experience among new cyclists is the "downpour epiphany." This typically happens the first time a rider gets caught in heavy rain. During an unexpected soaking, people normally tense up, curse their luck, and wish they were elsewhere. But on a bike, something mysterious happens; the experience of being rained on can be hugely enjoyable. Perhaps it's because the water is refreshing. Or just feels nice. Or because the world shimmers beautifully in the rain.

I think something more profound is involved, too. The downpour epiphany is partly about the release of apprehension that comes when the sky lets go and we realize it doesn't matter. We're so used to being screened off from the world, sometimes we forget the joys of getting out there and just *being* in it, firsthand, face-to-face. Cycling reminds us how.

Sometimes we forget the joys of getting out there and just being *in it, firsthand, face-to-face.*

BIKE TO REALITY

◆

As a boy, bikes and practical skills went hand in hand for me. One of my fondest childhood memories is of spending time in the garage with my dad teaching me how to fix my old BMX. Later, as a teenager, my "Muddyfox" mountain bike helped me complete a paper round every day before school. Occasionally I had to go on foot, for one reason or another, and trudging up the road with that heavy paper bag made me appreciate my bike even more. Looking back, I suppose I was a pretty industrious child. Then philosophy happened.

I T'S NOT THAT I STOPPED WORKING HARD. If anything, I worked even harder. But I was diverting my energies into problems without solutions. Such problems can be exhilaratingly interesting, but they can't be solved by practical skills. Or by cycling. There's nowhere you can go and nothing you can do to solve a problem without a solution.

As I progressed in my philosophical studies, I met a lot of relativists. One girl told me that my own body didn't actually exist—that it was, instead, just a matter of opinion. Some people I met seemed as if they had simply *forgotten* about the world. There was one guy who had no idea how to boil water. I'm not joking.

Suffice it to say, I wasn't fluent in reality by the time I completed my doctorate. Einstein once said he achieved his breakthroughs by standing on the shoulders of giants, but the only giants I ever stood on had their heads in the clouds. When, inevitably, I fell to earth with a bump, I had a lot to get my head around, and fast.

Luckily, rediscovering cycling helped me to learn five times faster. The realistic mindset that the bicycle encourages—practical, prepared, enterprising—soon blossomed in other areas of my life. I decided to start my own business, and, since cycling had been my inspiration, I founded *Cycle Lifestyle*, a free magazine promoting cycling. I had come full circle. I had ridden back to reality.

This is one of my favorite Zen verses. It's about a spiritual journey that ends with a down-to-earth appreciation of reality, but with the heightened joy of arriving home.

> *Misty rain on Mount Lu,*
> *And waves surging in Che-chaing:*
> *When you have not yet been there,*
> *Many a regret surely you have;*
> *But once there and homeward you wend,*
> *How matter of fact things look!*
> *Misty rain on Mount Lu,*
> *And waves surging in Che-chaing.*
> SU TUNG PO

CHAPTER TWO

$$E = mc^2$$

FREEWHEELING

Cycling nurtures an "individual" attitude
just like Einstein's. Through the childlike joy
of exploring freely, we rediscover our independence.
Exercising our bodies wakes up our minds, setting us
off on voyages of creativity and imagination. The
rhythm of the ride eases us into flow and inspires
us to greater determination. We are the rebels of the
road—freethinking, confident, expressive. We are
mindful of our potential, of who we can be.

STEPPING OUT

◆

A calm summer evening in Zurich was interrupted suddenly by piano music drifting from an old attic room. Next door, the greatest physicist of all time was studying quietly—he hadn't yet passed his college exams. As the young man's ears pricked up, he gathered himself out of his chair and strode from his lodgings toward the source of the disturbance, with his landlady in hot pursuit. "Herr Einstein," she cried, while he barreled up the stairs of his neighbor's house, brandishing a wooden object. When he burst through the door, an elderly lady looked up disconcertedly from her piano. "Go on playing," begged Einstein. As she did, he placed a bow onto the strings of his violin and played along. The sonata was Mozart's, but the moment belonged to Einstein—at his free-spirited, impudent, and creative best.

F REE-SPIRITEDNESS LENDS ITSELF TO IMPUDENCE. Impudence lends itself to creativity. Childhood is a time when these traits blossom, and Einstein's flowering was exceptional. Barely older than a toddler, he watched German troops parading through Munich. Kids were streaming onto the streets, eager to join the march, but the young Einstein was unimpressed. "When I grow up," he informed his parents, "I don't want to be one of those poor people."

The first figures of authority to encounter Einstein's free spirit were his teachers. One of them warned Einstein that his impertinence made him unwelcome in the classroom. Later, a college professor grumbled that "he always does something different from what I have ordered." As Einstein's brilliance became evident, others tried flattering him: "You're a very clever boy Einstein. An extremely clever boy. But you have one great fault: you'll never let yourself be told anything."

Einstein especially hated exams, which he thought destroyed curiosity. "One had to cram all this stuff into one's mind ... whether one liked it or not," he chided, adding that an "education based on free action and personal responsibility" is superior to "one relying on outward authority."

Never Grow Old

The young Einstein's free-spiritedness was remarkable not just in its intensity, but in its duration. "People like you and me never grow old," he wrote to a friend later in life. "We never cease to stand like curious children before the great mystery into which we were born."

Eventually, Einstein came to attribute some of his greatest scientific accomplishments to his enduringly naive approach. "The ordinary adult never bothers his head about the problems of space and time," he wrote. "These are things he has thought of as a child. But I developed so slowly that I began to wonder about space and time when I was already grown up. Consequently, I probed more deeply into the problem than an ordinary child would have."

In doing so, he took a risk no ordinary adult would have. Other contemporary theorists had nearly hit upon relativity, but they held back. Einstein had no such scruples. For one thing, he wasn't afraid of being wrong: "Anyone who has never made a mistake has never tried anything new." Nor was he afraid of defying tradition: "A foolish faith in authority is the worst enemy of truth." At times, Einstein positively reveled in rebellion, seeing it as his finest asset. "Long live impudence," he exclaimed, "it is my guardian angel in this world."

After his theories became well known, nothing much changed in Einstein's outlook. On one occasion, he gave a lecture in Prague (in today's Czech Republic), which was followed by several gushing speeches. He was invited to respond, and did—in his own irreverent way. "It will perhaps be pleasanter and more understandable," he suggested, "if instead of making a speech I play a piece for you on the violin." Einstein proceeded to serenade the astonished audience.

The Laughing Philosopher

Einstein's impudence was backed up by a mischievous sense of humor and a laugh like a wild animal. It seems he retained into adulthood a mild form of echolalia, which made him enjoy repeating silly phrases. No occasion, no matter how portentous, was above Einstein's playfulness. In one of the most famous letters in the history of science, he tipped off a friend about the four papers he would publish during his miracle year. "You frozen whale," he began, before apologizing for the "inconsequential babble" that was to follow. Years later, when Einstein was famous, he attended a reception where yet more long speeches were being waffled in his honor. Turning to a distinguished gentleman beside him, he joked sympathetically, "I've just developed a new theory of eternity."

Whether poking his tongue out at photographers, naming his own sailing boat *Tinef* (Yiddish for "piece of junk"), or piling earthenware in a friend's bed, Einstein was "a laughing philosopher, and his witty sarcasm mercilessly castigated all vanity and artificiality," as one classmate put it.

A Racing Mind

Of course, it wasn't all joking around with this genius. Einstein was determined to uncover the truth wherever he glimpsed it. To such a tenacious individual, coming first mattered. In 1915 he was locked in an incredible race with one of the outstanding mathematicians of the day, David Hilbert. A decade earlier, Einstein had published his "special" theory of relativity, so-called because it was applicable only in certain special situations. He had since been working on a "general" version of the theory—a tougher task. Over the years he had benefited from correspondence with many fine scholars who, like the leading pack in a long-distance race, sportingly cajoled each other to succeed. Now, with the finish in sight, Einstein and Hilbert had broken away.

Historians dispute who crossed the line first, but Hilbert graciously conceded priority to Einstein, who, after all, had come up with the idea and done most of the work. In the years surrounding the publication of his general theory of relativity, Einstein's productivity was astonishing. The result, his colleagues admitted, was "one of the greatest achievements of human thought," wrought in "arguably the most prodigious effort of sustained brilliance on the part of one man in the history of physics."

Strict Angels

In sustaining his efforts, Einstein engaged in many long periods of flow—that complete absorption in a task whereby you lose all sense of yourself and your surroundings. Being able to concentrate so intensely was not just good for Einstein's work, it was good for his mood. In 1903 he married a young physicist, Mileva Marić, but she soon became depressed and sick, as did their second son Eduard. Throughout these travails, Einstein sought refuge in the combined joys of studying nature and thinking hard. These, he held, were "the fortifying yet relentlessly strict angels that shall lead me through all of life's troubles."

He tried to instill in the listless Eduard the importance of keeping busy with meaningful projects. "Life is like riding a bicycle," said the concerned father. "To keep your balance, you must keep moving." Einstein was more qualified than most to make such a pronouncement, having experienced both the dejectedness of his early career, and the emptiness of success: "I love to travel," Einstein concluded, "but hate to arrive."

Cosmic Composer

No matter how strict your angels are, you don't win the Nobel Prize without a few brain cells to rub together. Behind Einstein's sparkling eyes was an electric mind, with an IQ estimated at greater than 160. However, one of Einstein's merits shone the brightest: his creativity. Out of his teeming imagination surged legions of powerful theories. His originality stunned a world that hadn't experienced such alchemy since Newton cast a spell over physics more than two centuries previously. *Warped space! Bending light rays! Time slowing down!* The hallmark of genius is the inexplicability of its provenance, and even Einstein was none the wiser when it came to that of his own theories. "If we knew what it was we were doing, it would not be called research, would it?" he quipped.

Einstein did know how to give his creativity a helping hand. "A new intuition" is "nothing but the outcome of earlier intellectual experience," he remarked. Yet Einstein also knew that it tends to be during breaks from learning or hard work that eureka moments come. Archimedes famously had his while relaxing in a bathtub (before he ran naked into the street). Newton allegedly conceived of gravity while resting under an apple tree. "A new idea comes *suddenly*," Einstein recognized; when we're in the present, thinking about nothing in particular, gently mindful of our experience, marvelous things can happen.

However, sitting around waiting wasn't Einstein's style. Instead, he practiced the violin—a more active kind of resting. The rhythm of the bowing; the harmony of the strings; the vitality of the melodies; all these seemed to resonate in Einstein's subconscious, stirring it into imaginative activity that would soon burst out like a chorus. His violin helped him get in flow, too. Nothing flows more than a great piece of music. By helping Einstein to focus and imagine, playing music primed him for great feats of intellectual discovery. No wonder he carried his battered violin case wherever he went.

The Outsider

Einstein had a lifelong aversion to any form of authoritarianism, militarism, or nationalism—whether fascist or communist. He hated anything that involved a herd mentality, always championing instead the sacredness of individual choice— free speech, free action. "The most important mission of the state," he insisted, "is to protect the individual and to make it possible for him to develop into a creative personality." He added, "Only the individual can produce the new ideas."

Sadly, history had other ideas. In 1933 Hitler seized power in Germany, and Einstein, an ethnic Jew, was forced to flee his homeland as Nazism started on its devastating course. It was a timely escape; shortly afterward, Einstein discovered that he had been listed for assassination. His great scientific feats had only served to inflame the Nazis; mobs were burning books and castigating intellectualism as some kind of Jewish disease. Thankfully, one of Einstein's friends salvaged his scientific papers—an act that symbolizes the triumph of freedom in its darkest hour. For the rest of his life, Einstein campaigned avidly for democracy, freedom, and peace.

GOING IT ALONE

In a park in East London in June 1983, a momentous event took place. It was attended by few. A New Zealander, male, with longish bowl-cut hair, tattered flared jeans and a colorful checkered shirt; an Australian, female, with an impressive curly bouffant, wearing a look of gentle anxiety on her face; three children, scampering around like huskies, excited, anticipating something; and a real dog, brown and white, sniffing a tree, oblivious to what was about to go down.

TIME SEEMED TO STAND STILL. Suddenly, they all gasped (apart from the dog). It was happening. A small boy wearing a superman T-shirt hurtled down a grassy hill, then veered back up the other side, before wobbling to a halt in a crumpled but triumphant pile, the back wheel of his red bicycle still spinning. The youngest of the Irvine family had experienced his first taste of freedom.

That was my first bike ride, and I bet you can still remember yours. If you're my age, you probably started out on a bike with training wheels—extra wheels attached to the rear hub. These would have been removed when you became confident enough. Then, it was a case of getting a running push from an adult, and just going with it. The moment you realized you were riding on your own never seems to fade from memory.

These days "balance bikes" are popular. Like little running machines, they don't have pedals. Kids get used to the sensation of balancing before swapping onto a proper bike. The end result, though, is the same: unforgettable exhilaration.

What makes that first bike ride so special? Kids love independence, and cycling allows them to explore farther and faster than they ever thought possible—discovering just how much freedom a bicycle allows is quite a thrill. Children also love the pride that comes with emulating grown-ups and acquiring new skills—it feels incredible to do something as impressive as balancing. When you add in the suddenness and singularity of a child's first ride (compared to, say, learning to read, which doesn't have an obvious finale), the excitement is exquisite. It is rarely surpassed, in memory as in life.

Big Kids

Just as freedom makes kids on bikes feel independent, it makes adults on bikes feel like kids again. Anyone who cycles regularly will agree: every now and then cycling stirs up feelings of nostalgic euphoria, otherwise inspired only by rainbows, shooting stars, and fireworks.

It's easy to see why. Compared to other modes of transport, cycling makes people feel as though a burden has been lifted from their shoulders. There are no traffic jams to worry about: bikes trickle through. Delays and cancellations on public transportation don't matter: bikes aren't scheduled. Crowds and waiting lines are irrelevant: bikes are elsewhere. The only burden on your bike is you.

And the rest is up to you. A bike can take you via a secret back alley or quiet side street, along a pretty riverside path, across a lonely bridge, in bus lanes, over paving stones, on a mountain track or a trail in the woods, past mansions or trailer parks, through puddles, into the suburbs, uptown, down country lanes, along a disused railroad line, and through the park. Perhaps even in a single ride!

With so many hidden gems to discover, too far off the beaten track to walk, drive, or take public transportation to, cycling rewards exploration and curiosity. It also encourages such expansiveness by giving people the confidence to undertake journeys that might otherwise have come with a feeling of vulnerability. This applies in time as well as space. Late at night or early in the morning, when darkness and loneliness conspire, a bike provides reassurance, like a motherly attachment figure, or a guardian angel. Freedom and cycling go hand in hand.

Going on a Bike Ride

Cycling is such a great way to get from point A to point B, people sometimes forget you can ride aimlessly. As the old Zen proverb puts it: "I ride my bicycle to ride my bicycle."

You probably did this thousands of times as a kid—cycling wherever your fancy took you, just "going on a bike ride." Why not try it again one day, when the traffic is light and you've no other commitments?

As you go along slowly, see if you have any impulses to plan your route, head toward somewhere in particular, or speed up. Let these thoughts pass by like clouds. Notice them—but don't judge them. Gently bring your attention back to the present moment, so you can decide where to go *when you go*.

Maybe you'll nose down a side street into a dead end. Who cares? Maybe you'll find a stream in a wood and an old wooden bridge with "Debbie loves John" carved into it. Who knows? Maybe you'll get lost. Who dares? Going on a bike ride is fun, and it's a different adventure every time.

There's also something liberating about the actual physical sensation of cycling. As the nature writer Louis J. Halle noted, riding a bike may be the closest a human being comes to experiencing flight—not just *being flown*, as on a plane, but *actually flying*, like a bird. Cyclists can swoop downhill with a majestic aerial view, pedal steadily like a migrating bird flapping, alternate between rapid effort and gliding, or weave a deft trajectory through an urban jungle.

Free Your Mind

Playing his violin was just one kind of active resting Einstein engaged in. He also did a lot of creative thinking while sailing, although his skills as a sailor were as ropy as his boat. There are numerous tales of him falling in the water and being rescued.

Most famous of all, however, is the active resting Einstein did on his bicycle. He was cycling when he first imagined what it would be like to ride alongside a beam of light. This got him thinking about how motion influences our perceptions of space and time. He soon made some startling discoveries. For instance, if I cycle past you, our motion relative to each other has a peculiar consequence; you will perceive that, where I am, time slows down and space contracts. Einstein's relativity equations described the complex relationships that connect time, space, motion, mass, and our observations.

If that made your head spin, don't worry. The point is that cycling made Einstein's head spin in a whirl of creativity. Even as an old man, having settled in Princeton, New Jersey, after fleeing the Nazis, Einstein's bicycle was an important source of active rest for him. He could often be seen riding around the university campus, the rhythm of the pedals giving him the same imaginative boost as bowing his violin.

Tuning in

Not everyone can think up the theory of relativity while on a bicycle, but they *can* experience the astonishing surge in creativity that pedaling brings. It really is astonishing. The difference between your mental ecology before and during a ride is like tuning a radio from static to crystal clear. Instead of having vague and fleeting impressions against a background of anxiety-inducing fuzz that stops you from latching onto anything meaningful, new ideas come lucidly, with ease.

The thing about creativity is that it's unpredictable—novel thoughts by definition have unexpected content. This can be wonderfully useful. Cyclists often experience a theater of lightbulb moments while riding. *That's the solution! Here's what I need to do! This would work!* With a mind surging so wildly, the hardest thing to do is remember all those helpful ideas when the ride is over.

But the flipside of all this novelty is the downright weirdness of many cycling-inspired imaginings. Strange concatenations of words and images come drifting through your consciousness like those surreal-looking iridescent fish that live in the deep ocean. Sometimes, a pointless snippet of a melody or a ditty pops in and out of your head. Then it pops

The thing about creativity is that it's unpredictable—novel thoughts by definition have unexpected content.

in again. And again. Creativity doesn't care if you think its offerings are bizarre, or even annoying. It does what it likes, as many times as it likes. In fact, it seems to revel in being rude. One imaginary chorus my mind decided to tune into while I was riding was "Bugger me, it's Puckeridge."

Not all the mind-music inspired by cycling is annoying. Sometimes a melody occurs to you, real or otherwise, that is so vivid and enjoyable you feel compelled to sing it aloud—often ecstatically. It seems that, just as the rhythms of music and pedaling inspire creativity, the rhythms of pedaling inspire musicality.

This is the beauty of cycling—the rhythm puts

serious activity in the brain to sleep: it creates a void.

Random thoughts enter that void—the chorus from

a song, a verse of poetry, a detail in the countryside,

a joke, the answer to something that vexed me long ago.

FROM "IT'S ALL ABOUT THE BIKE" BY ROBERT PENN
PARTICULAR BOOKS, 2010

All this cycling-inspired creativity may be part of the explanation for why cyclists don't tend to be narcissistic about their bikes and other material objects. Instead of expressing themselves indirectly, through fashionable products, cyclists become creative enough to express themselves directly, through artistic, scientific, or entrepreneurial pursuits.

FLOW MOTION

◆

It comes on gradually then suddenly, induced by the spinning of the wheels, the rhythm of the pedaling, or the landscape projecting out of the distance then careening over your shoulders. When flow happens, nothing matters except you, your bike, and your journey. No thoughts knock on your mind. Your feelings busy themselves; the world is just right. There are few better sensations than cycling in flow.

JUST AS PLAYING THE VIOLIN helped Einstein work on physics by honing his concentration, cycling helps you get in the right frame of mind for performing mental tasks. When you get off your bike, you are invariably more alert yet calm, and contented yet focused, than you were before you got on. Flow keeps flowing, making the rest of your day go more smoothly.

Rolling On

Sometimes cycling seems unappealing. When the wind blows hard and the rain comes sideways, it can be tempting to find another way to travel. Either that or just stay in. However, bicycles reward hardiness. In bad weather, you may need a hat and gloves to keep your extremities comfortable, but the rest of your body gets snug within minutes of pedaling. While other people are breathing fog over disrupted train schedules, shivering beneath frosty windshields, or grimacing in wind-swept bus shelters, cyclists cruise, energized and warm.

Even when you just feel tired or downtrodden, cycling picks you up. When you're drifting, it gives you direction. When you're struggling, it gives you momentum. When you're flagging, it gives you a boost. All it takes is one small effort to get started, and your bike will do the rest. Cycling escalates a flicker of determination as a cathedral amplifies a whisper. And the best thing is, the enhanced determination brought about by cycling lasts throughout your day, just as flow keeps on flowing after you've dismounted.

The Race

My friend Adam once got so psyched up on his bike, he basically started racing against himself. It's a game—he calls it "The Race"—which is more fun than it sounds. The rules are simple. You start out with a score of zero. For every cyclist you overtake, it goes up by one, and for every cyclist who overtakes you, it goes down by one. You win when you finish your journey in credit; you lose when your score is negative.

If you play this game, you'll soon find yourself inventing rules for contentious situations. For instance, if you've overtaken a cyclist who's waiting to turn right, do you still earn a point? The point is, The Race is extraordinarily engrossing. By strengthening your determined streak, cycling makes you want to be the best you can.

Road Rebels

Ever since the pioneering days of cycling, the public majority's attitude toward cyclists has ranged from indifference via irritation to indignation. Why this is the case is something of a mystery. You'd think that people everywhere would welcome with open arms an affordable vehicle that alleviates congestion on streets and public transportation, reduces noise and air pollution, and hardly ever harms pedestrians.

Alas not. Being a cyclist often means going against the grain, so a thick skin and a rebellious streak are required from the outset. Once you're on your way, though, you find that your impudence grows with every rotation of the pedals. A pedestrian distracted by a smartphone waddles insensately into your path, gets startled, then glares at you. You rise above it. A driver ravaged by stress leans out of a nearside window and, like a rabid dog barking at a butterfly, rants in your wake as you nip through stationary traffic. You're glad you didn't take the car. A fashion victim waiting at a bus stop sneers at your luminous jacket, then gets splashed by a passing motorcycle. You smile mischievously.

By the time you finish your cycle journey, you just *know* you made the right choice, never mind the opposers, and it's a feeling of assurance and conviction that infuses the rest of your day. Sometimes you encounter the same boorish looks you got while you were on your bike when you're off it. Whatever the issue may be, you feel ready to stand up for yourself when you see those looks. The impudence you get from cycling is long-lived, indeed.

Cyclists Will Inherit the Earth

If you ever get into a debate with someone who dislikes cycling, two things are highly probable. First, your inter-locutor won't actually have ridden a bike for years. Second, he or she will attempt, on the brink of losing the argument, to land one last flailing blow on you: "At the end of the day, cycling is just far too dangerous."

A lot of cyclists are indeed somewhat gung ho. With all the scaremongering surrounding cycling, most people wouldn't get on a bike in the first place unless they were more spirited than your average Joe. But just because risk takers cycle, it doesn't mean that all cyclists take a risk. If you plan your route properly, you can travel along quiet streets (or parks), where trucks and buses, the biggest threats, can't fit. These mild and pleasant trips are about as dangerous as, well, just being alive in general.

In fact, this may be a massive understatement, even when applied to all cycle journeys. Studies show that cycling pro-tects against heart disease, stroke, obesity, dementia, diabetes, high blood pressure, and some cancers, while supporting healthy bones, muscles, joints, and even sleep patterns. These benefits are the same for most kinds of physical exercise, but cycling is an especially worthy pursuit because it has a minimal tendency to cause overuse injuries, and can be seamlessly incorporated into your daily schedule as a useful mode of transport. Another great thing about exercising on a bike is that you can work as hard or as lightly as you want, or even take a break by coasting along for a while.

When you're turning the crankset,

you're riding the bike. When you're coasting,

you're just along for the ride.

NED OVEREND (1955–)
MOUNTAIN BIKING CHAMPION

One report has summarized that the risks involved in cycling are "minimal" and "are outweighed by the health benefits by a factor of around twenty to one" (*Cycling and Health*, 2007). Now, newcomers should be aware of the importance of safe cycling (above all, they should never ride to the right of a vehicle that is signaling right or turning right), but if I could convince non-cyclists of one thing it would be that finding. Even better, I'd tell them to go out and ride. "The bicycle," as the American cycling advocate Richard Ballantine notes, "is its own best argument."

The Joy of Cycling

Have you ever been in a bad mood, but then something amusing happens and you can't keep a straight face, no matter how hard you try? I was once accused of cheating in a game of pool and was complaining afterward to someone else about this injustice. I meant to say "I'm noble" (which was ludicrous enough), but what actually came out was "I'm a nobleman." After a pause, the two of us exchanged a puzzled look, then cracked up with laughter. I am certainly not a nobleman.

Cycling has a similar effect on negativity—the two simply don't go together. Just as it's hard to be solemn on a pogo stick, meditative on a rodeo horse, or presidential on a Segway, it's almost impossible to be in a bad mood on a bike. The only mood associated with cycling is happiness, a positive feeling that persists even after you leave the saddle. It's as if your gloom simply evaporates as you pedal. Studies bear this out, showing that cyclists are protected against various mental disorders, including depression, anxiety, and low self-esteem. This is partly due to the fact that a healthy body leads to a healthy mind (both of which are promoted by endorphins— hormones released by exercise), but there are plenty of other reasons why bicycles make us happy.

Cycling brings many of the causes of happiness under your personal control. The pleasures of learning, for instance, become easier to attain because cycling boosts your intelligence. In the environment in which human beings evolved, physical exertion often meant traveling to a different place. This favored in our ancestors a tendency to be sensitive to new information and ideas after exercising. Today, our brains retain this design feature, so cycling makes us better learners, which makes us happier. Contrary to the popular myth that clever people are uptight, they actually lead comparatively more expansive and rewarding lives.

Then there are the financial benefits of cycling. Once you've purchased a bike and factored in the minimal costs of maintenance (about $120 per year at a local repair shop), there are huge savings to be made: on tickets for trains or buses (and other miscellaneous outlays on public transportation, including newspapers and takeout coffees), or on driving costs, such as gasoline, maintenance, and parking fees. In a recession more than ever, cycling boosts happiness by reducing financial stress.

Security is another cause of happiness that a bicycle brings under your personal control. Compared to the haphazardness of other means of transport, cycling is regular, reliable, and predictable. Your bicycle won't cancel on you, trap you in traffic, make you wait around in the midnight gloom, or have you anxiously biting your nails because the government has told you to amplify your alertness levels when using public transportation. Cycling offers riders familiarity and certainty, crucial components of a securely happy mind.

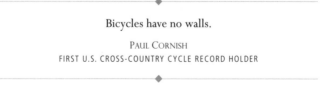

Bicycles have no walls.

PAUL CORNISH
FIRST U.S. CROSS-COUNTRY CYCLE RECORD HOLDER

No Walls

The train slows. Shunts forward. Picks up speed. Then crawls again. Stops. Heart quickens. Blackened tunnel walls. Pipes running horizontally, inches from murky windows. Train lights flicker. Darkness. Heart pounding. Lights back on. Heart still pounding. Passengers check watches. Legs feel weak. No empty seats. Fabric against face. A coat. Smells like old carpet, a sink full of dirty washing. Palms sweaty. Too hot. Can't get off. Heart thumping. Engine growls. Yes! Then stops. Tinny drum machine leaks from someone's earphones. Try the doors? Don't be stupid. Head's thumping now. Heart shaking like a fist. We're moving! Driver apologizes. Moving fast now. Relief, like a waterfall. Pipes blurring. Never-ending pipes. Suddenly, a sea of light. People, briefcases, advertising posters. Arrive at the station. Made it.

Every day, millions of people experience the stress of traveling on a subway or train system. When those trains stop in tunnels, personally I'd rather be anywhere else on earth. While I lived in London, cycling was my escape ticket from the "Tube" (London's underground system), and these days, when I go back, I always take my bike. It's all about the freedom. As a cyclist you can go wherever you like, whenever you like. Compared to those doom-filled tunnels, London's streets are like alpine vistas. Compared to staring at those grim pipes, I feel like I'm riding alongside a beam of light. Tunnel vision, incapacitation, and stress are replaced by creativity, determination, and happiness. I wrote this book not just about cycling, but *by* cycling.

CHAPTER THREE

$$E = {}_m c^2$$

AROUND
THE BLOCK

*Cycling fosters a "local" attitude just like
Einstein's. In choosing an unpretentious mode
of transport and plain attire, we realize the simple
virtues of modesty and humility. Out and about, we
get to know our local area and our communities better;
face to face, we're approachable and sociable, friendlier
and kinder. We empathize with our neighbors and
appreciate the value of inclusivity and equality.
In being mindful of others, we help create a
more pleasant environment for everyone.*

HERE I AM

◆

It was Einstein's birthday, and his friends in Bern had prepared a surprise meal for him. He had met Maurice Solovine, a philosophy student, and Conrad Habicht, a mathematics graduate, a few months earlier. The young trio had since convened regularly to discuss physics and philosophy, and had satirically dubbed themselves "The Olympia Academy." Instead of their usual dinner of sausages, cheese, tea, and fruit, on Einstein's special day there were three plates of caviar on the table. As he swallowed handfuls, and rhapsodized about Galileo, his fellow diners exchanged amused looks. "Do you know what you've been eating?" Solovine hinted, finally. "For goodness sake!" Einstein whooped. "So that was the famous caviar! Well, if you offer gourmet food to peasants like me, you know they won't appreciate it." He did, of course, appreciate his friends. With his modest outlook and simple tastes, Einstein valued people all the more.

SEVERAL YEARS LATER, THE OLYMPIA ACADEMY'S finest thinker was beginning to attract attention. Einstein's "miracle year" flurry of revolutionary publications had generally fallen on deaf ears, but a few alert physicists had taken note. One of these was Max Planck, a giant in the field. He and Einstein began corresponding in 1906, and the professor promised to visit Bern. As it turned out, he sent his assistant, Max Laue, who was surprised to learn that Einstein was not an academic. And that was only the half of it.

They arranged to meet in the reception area of Einstein's workplace, but when the excited patent officer came downstairs there was seemingly no one waiting for him. Laue recalled: "The young man who came to meet me made so unexpected an impression on me that I did not believe he could possibly be the father of the relativity theory ... so I let him pass." Only when Einstein returned did Laue realize his mistake.

Down to Earth

With his baggy clothing, too-short pants, casual grooming, uncombed hair, and lack of socks, Einstein resembled a struggling artist rather than a great scientist. He retained this down-to-earth look long after his achievements became well known. In 1909, when he was offered an honorary doctorate to commemorate the founding of Geneva University, Einstein attended the presentation ceremony wearing a straw hat.

Few occasions were above his sartorial indifference. When his second wife, Elsa Löwenthal, implored him to wear something smart to meet the German ambassador and his coterie, Einstein shot back: "They want to see me. Here I am. If they want to see my clothes, open my closet and show them my suits."

Plain Living

It wasn't just plain attire that pleased Einstein, but plain living. "You have no idea how charming such a life with very small needs and without grandeur can be," he wrote to Elsa. His simple tastes were reflected in the unassuming spaces he inhabited—including, at the height of his fame, the modest house the couple bought in Princeton and lived in happily for twenty-one years.

Even when grander surroundings were readily available, Einstein often shunned them. In a rented house on Long Island, he ate in the pantry because the dining hall was too extravagant. In a hotel in New York, he blocked off half his apartment because it was too spacious. And he frequently opted to travel in third class on the train, despite having a first-class ticket.

I Am Indebted

Einstein's unaffected style and simple tastes epitomized his humility toward people in general. Not one to show off in front of others, he was unpretentious, unceremonious, and honest, even as his fame skyrocketed. When a worried girl wrote to him about her schoolwork, his response was characteristic: "Do not be concerned over your difficulties in mathematics. I can assure you that mine are even greater."

As a lecturer, Einstein remained no less affable, regularly pausing to check that his students were keeping up and inviting them to interject. Such familiarity was a rare thing in academia, and it didn't go unnoticed at Zurich University. Before he transferred to Prague University, his students compiled a petition, pointing out that "it is a great delight for us to follow his lectures, and he is so good at establishing a perfect rapport with his audience."

Einstein was pleasant to assistants and colleagues alike, always treating people respectfully whether they agreed with him or not. And when intellectual credit was due, he was quick to grant it. Indeed, his first paper on relativity concludes with a tribute: "Let me note that my friend and colleague M. Besso steadfastly stood by me in my work on the problem discussed here, and that I am indebted to him for several valuable suggestions."

For Einstein, modesty was an instinct but also a virtue. "I consider that plain living is good for everybody, physically and mentally," he wrote. In Geneva it wasn't just his hat that made this point. The university had been founded in 1559 by John Calvin, a notoriously austere fellow. Yet the ostentatious parade and formal dinner Einstein attended spared no expense. He turned to a distinguished-looking guest and murmured, "Do you know what Calvin would have done had he been here? He would have erected an enormous stake and had us all burned for our sinful extravagance." Later, Einstein recollected that "the man never addressed another word to me."

Give to Others Much

Despite his staunch intellectual independence, Einstein led a convivial life. He loved socializing, whether playing music in a group or discussing ideas, preferably with a cup of coffee in one hand and a cheap cigar in the other. His friendships were deep and rewarding, sometimes lasting for decades or, in the case of Solovine and Habicht, a lifetime. Strangers warmed to him. "I was particularly struck," said a fellow physicist, "by his mild and thoughtful expression, by his general kindness, by his simplicity and his friendliness."

Einstein's generosity was especially endearing. In 1902 he placed an advertisement in a local newspaper in Bern, offering his services as a physics tutor. A young philosophy student spied it eagerly. The following day, Einstein received a knock on his door. It was Maurice Solovine. They hit it off immediately and agreed to meet again. On their third meeting, Einstein insisted on waiving the tuition fee because he was enjoying the sessions so much.

Wherever he went, he made time for the local community. When an eight-year-old girl visited his house in Princeton and asked for help with her math homework, he obliged—she had, after all, brought him some fudge. Soon she was turning up regularly with the same request. Her parents were mortified when they found out, but Einstein said he didn't mind.

On another occasion, he granted an interview to a struggling journalism student who had written saying he was hopeful of an A grade if he could land such a prestigious assignment. Einstein even agreed to pose for a portrait by a friend's wife whose artistic talents were questionable. Why did he do it? "Because she's a nice woman," he explained.

A Full Life

Einstein's kindness and intelligence proved to be a popular combination. Throughout his life—married or otherwise, it seems—he was never short of romantic interests. The photographs by which he is best known today capture something of his lovable eccentricity, but not his youthful handsomeness. He had "masculine good looks of the type that played havoc at the turn of the century," as one female friend put it.

Mileva Marić, Einstein's first wife, saw him at his most intense and intimate. His family disapproved of her, which seemed to inspire his passion further. When the two lovers married, Mileva's father offered Einstein money, but he declined, saying he had not married Mileva for that reason. Miloš Marić was deeply touched.

Einstein tried his best to be a good father. "My husband often spends his free time at home just playing with the boy," wrote Mileva, after their first son, Hans Albert, was born. Their second son, Eduard, arrived a few years later, and the whole family, joined by Einstein's sister Maria, would go on bike rides together.

After the marriage degenerated, in part due to Mileva's depressive temperament, Einstein continued to correspond with his family and provide for them financially. While racing to complete his general theory of relativity, he still found the time to write heart-wrenching personal letters to his estranged wife and disillusioned sons, hoping that he could somehow smooth things over. When Eduard, too, became mired in a lonely depression, Einstein penned some touching words of encouragement: "People who live in a society, enjoy looking into each other's eyes, who share their troubles, who focus their efforts on what is important to them and find this joyful—these people lead a full life."

The Most Valuable Thing

There is a dubious cliché that says that scientists are too concerned with the minutiae of equations and material things to care about people. Not Einstein. He knew the value of human relationships. This was evidenced in his compassionate political outlook—one of his greatest heroes was Gandhi. With an inbuilt sense of fairness, Einstein hated class divisions and inequality. "Striving for social justice is the most valuable thing to do in life," he declared.

The most important human endeavor
is the striving for morality in our actions.

EINSTEIN

To this end, he wrote and spoke extensively and lent his support to hundreds of humanitarian organizations and campaign groups. His second wife Elsa charged a dollar for his autograph and five dollars for his photograph. They donated the proceeds to children's charities.

Einstein was particularly passionate about defending the equality of all races. On his arrival in the United States, he was horrified by the racial segregation he encountered. He joined the National Association for the Advancement of Colored People and became a champion of civil liberties, declaring racism to be "America's worst disease." When Marian Anderson, a black contralto singer, was refused a room in a Princeton hotel while performing in the town, Einstein made a public show of inviting her to stay with him. They became friends.

FRIENDLY LOCAL LIVING

Have you ever taken a trip down memory lane? It's a pleasant journey. Birds sing. Kids play outside. Old ladies chat at the bus stop. A man in his front yard prunes roses. A school crossing guard waits for children. Church bells ring for a wedding. Flowers are displayed outside a store. A police officer gives directions to a passerby. The smell of fresh bread drifts from the bakery. A dog walker calls and whistles in the park. Youngsters play soccer, using sweaters for goalposts. An ice cream van turns the corner. Neighbors talk over a fence. And the best thing about memory lane is that you can cycle there any time you like.

DO YOU KNOW WHERE YOU LIVE? I don't mean the name of the place you live in, I mean the place itself. Probably you know some landmarks and various useful locations—

On a bike you tend
to observe details that would
otherwise slip through the cracks
of your awareness.

the supermarket, the doctors' office, the train station—as
well as the streets that connect them. In this way, our local
environments are like webs that we navigate on autopilot.

Compare this to reading a book. In one sense, the two
abilities are similar. The meanings of words, phrases, and par-
agraphs point us toward various conclusions as we navigate
through the text on autopilot. But clearly there's more
to reading than this. When we immerse ourselves in the contents of a book we remain curious and alert, as watchful as a
scuba diver. While moving through the written environment
we notice little things. We read between the lines. We are
active but mindful.

In this sense, do you know where you live? If not, cycling
can help you to find out more. On a bike, you're not screened
off from the world as you are in a car or on public transportation, so you tend to observe details that would otherwise slip
through the cracks of your awareness. As well as moving
toward your destination, you savor the journey. As well as
traveling on autopilot, you stay canny. Cycling lends itself to
mindful going, a richer way of experiencing your local area.

MINDFUL GOING

❋

Being on a bike heightens your local awareness—as though the objects, people, and scenes you encounter are illuminated by spotlights. You pass by, but you take it all in.

Through deliberate meditation, you can really relish the experience of mindful going.

As you ride, try to focus on your surroundings in the same intense way that you've learned to focus on your breathing. You'll find that your eyes dart around—that's fine. These movements are as automatic as breathing is. The idea is not to focus on *only* one thing in your surroundings; this would be impossible, because you'll be on the move. The idea is to focus on anything your eyes happen to settle on.

See if you can maintain this focus and not get distracted by any thoughts, sensations, and feelings you have. Perhaps you'll see something that triggers an old memory, makes you feel a certain way, or gets you thinking. Try to let these reactions go. Notice them, but then bring your attention gently back to what you can see. Allow your surroundings to reveal themselves to you. Your only contribution is your curiosity.

Take in the little details. A car with a cracked license plate. Birds fighting in a tree. Aftershave. The dimples on a manhole cover. A child jumping in a puddle. Laundry hanging from the windows above a store. The smell of a barbecue. A quirky hairstyle. A dog barking. A lot of dogs barking back. An old man drinking a cup of coffee. The color of the sky.

When you cycle, these familiar sights become enthralling, as if part of a huge kaleidoscope.

Around Our Way

In bringing our surroundings alive, cycling helps us get to know our local communities better. On a bike you really notice your fellow citizens. Faces light up, body movements catch your eye, voices ring out. Generic matchstick people become high-res human beings, with all their individual characteristics and intriguing quirks.

Sometimes when you're on a bike and a passerby catches your eye, you smile at each other. Sometimes a fellow cyclist talks to you while you wait for the traffic lights to turn green. Other times you just enjoy the sense of belonging that comes from being out and about among people. It's especially great to feel this way while accomplishing the mundane activity of getting from point A to point B. Wherever you're going, cycling brings a communal spirit to the experience.

One of my favorite examples of this is cycling to watch a sports game. I'm always amazed that more home fans don't ride to see their team in action. After all, a huge part of the day's enjoyment is the atmosphere before the game, and on a bike you can really soak it up. While supporters mosey through the streets in a collage of shirts and hats, the air fills with a mixture of excitement and the aroma of hotdogs. Whereas drivers and public transportation users only catch the culmination of this pilgrimage, cyclists experience the full buildup, witnessing a trickle of fans grow into a river as the stadium nears.

The Joy of Commuting

There's one kind of journey that, more than any other, is enhanced by the communal pleasures of cycling: commuting. Studies suggest that getting to and from work is the unhappiest time of the day for most noncyclists. In 2004, the BBC (the British public broadcasting service) reported that in London, drivers and train passengers often experience more stress than a fighter pilot or a riot policeman going into action.

Part of the reason for such extreme stress is that these kinds of commute can be socially alienating. Traffic jams send drivers into solitary confinement. Rush-hour trains, at the other end of the scale, dehumanize their occupants by jamming them together awkwardly, like slaves in the hull of a ship, or migrants stowed in the back of a truck.

In contrast, as you cycle unimpeded through the bustle, you become involved in it, with a meaningful part to play. Yet it's also a feeling of novelty—as though you were skating alongside friendly strangers gathered on a frozen lake. Every day, cycling renews your sense of community and purpose.

And, like all bicycle-inspired moods, this one tends to stay with you, like momentum. Naturally, this is most noticeable in the morning. Not only does cycling to work bring you psychological rewards as an individual, it also makes you better disposed to your colleagues and your responsibilities. Studies confirm this, showing that commuting by bicycle improves employee morale and loyalty, and reduces absenteeism.

Just Hanging Out

How did I come to be sprawled on the grass with my limbs tangled up in the frame of my bike, my bare buttocks hanging out of my tracksuit pants, and my five best friends surrounding me, tears in their eyes, rolling around with laughter? Well, the short explanation is that I tried to jump over a ditch on a bicycle when I was 15 years old. My friends had managed it successfully, so I thought it would be easy enough for me. Unfortunately, I didn't "wheelie" over the edge—I assumed I was going fast enough to soar over like Evel Knievel, the famous stunt man. I was wrong. When my front wheel hit the far edge of the ditch, the bike and I turned a few somersaults before coming to an undamaged, albeit undignified, stop. That would have been the end of it if one of my pals hadn't ecstatically observed that my bicycle had conspired to pull my pants down during the tumble. "It's pulled his pants down!" was the last coherent thing anyone said for a good ten minutes.

So much for the short explanation. There's a deeper reason I have this (kind of) happy memory. My friends and I regularly used to hang out on bikes, and get up to all kinds of antics, so we were bound to have memorable experiences. I could tell you about the time I accidentally rode into a small river. Or about the "get lost" rides we went on in Epping Forest, near London, where the idea was, obviously, to get lost. Or about when we were chased by a pizza delivery man on his motor-cycle. I can assure you no one provoked him first. Honest.

These experiences show that, as well as being a sociable way of getting around, cycling is also a great way to socialize. It may sound like a juvenile thing to do, but why shouldn't adults, too, have fun hanging out on bikes? There's no age limit to the feeling of camaraderie that comes from riding to the beach or woods, racing through parks, exploring on a bike, or just stopping for refreshments or to say hi. And, of course, you can also meet new people on the way.

◆

Bicycles are almost as good as guitars for meeting girls.

BOB WEIR (1947–)
GUITARIST, SINGER AND FOUNDER MEMBER OF THE GRATEFUL DEAD

◆

Made for Two

Bikes are so much fun that they have a habit of creating a bond between people who cycle together—happy, shared memories make long-lasting friendships. But there's one emotional tie that cycling is best known for fostering: love.

You don't have to go to Paris to see why. Just about anywhere feels romantic when you cycle there with someone special. Maybe it's the spontaneity, the sense of "you and me against the world," the youthful high-spiritedness, the racing heart, or the rosy glow that comes with riding around in the fresh air. Or maybe it's just the thought of snuggling up on the couch at the end of an active day. Who knows? With characteristic mystery, love is conjured up by cycling, and the experience can be relived anywhere, anytime, reenergizing your relationship over and over.

Contrary to popular opinion, you don't need to be on a tandem to cycle romantically. Riding a two-seater, it turns out, is surprisingly arduous, especially for the so-called "stoker" sitting behind, who has to pedal while staring at someone else's back and resisting the temptation to tug on the immovable rear handlebars (doing so makes the bike topple over). This effort is part of the ongoing challenge both riders face in cooperating to keep the bike balanced; let's just say tandems are not nicknamed "divorce bikes" for nothing. Granted, there's a special charm in cycling *à deux*, but with separate bikes the romance comes easier; couples can share amorous glances, talk more easily, and keep out of ditches.

Daisy, Daisy,

Give me your answer, do.

I'm half crazy,

All for the love of you.

It won't be a stylish marriage –

I can't afford a carriage.

But you'll look sweet upon the seat

Of a bicycle built for two!

FROM "DAISY BELL"
HARRY DACRE, 1892

HERE I AM, CYCLING

◆

Einstein's temperament went hand in hand with his enjoyment of cycling. Even when automobiles were readily available, he chose to get around Princeton by bike. And because his pants were too short, they never got stuck in the chain.

MOTORIZED ROAD VEHICLES make their drivers feel self-important. It happens to all of us. Sitting in a luxurious, high-tech cockpit controlling a big, shiny, fast machine gives us a sense of entitlement, at least subconsciously. This conceit makes it hard not to view other road users as pesky obstacles (pedestrians or cyclists) or challengers (other drivers).

In contrast, cycling fosters a more modest mindset. On a bike, you're at close quarters with other road users, more of a participant than an overlord. You encounter pedestrians and fellow cyclists directly and openly—face to face, eye to eye —and you work together to keep out of each other's way. Good cyclists also communicate their intentions and make their presence known to drivers through frequent eye contact and other human gestures, such as waving and nodding. Diligently sharing the road fosters humility and empathy.

As well as conveying these various orienting signals, cyclists often communicate a message about themselves. Or rather, the message is that there is no message. Just as cyclists rarely seek to aggrandize themselves through narcissistically

posing on a particular mount—a bike is a bike—their clothing, too, typically indicates nothing about them. Cycling,
after all, is a practical activity, so it lends itself to practical
clothing—clothes that are, well, just clothes. That's not to say
you can't wear trendy designer outfits on a bike—it's just that
these wouldn't be the most practical choice. In getting into
the habit of wearing sensible clothes (or even geeky Lycra
outfits), cyclists again decline to show off in front of others.

◆

Nothing compares to the simple pleasure of a bike ride.

JOHN F. KENNEDY (1917–1963)
PRESIDENT FROM 1961 TO 1963

◆

Anyone Can Ride a Bike

Cycling cultivates a modest outlook and simple tastes, both
on and off the bike. Many cyclists, for instance, come to enjoy
wearing practical clothing even on days when they don't ride.
They come to value the relaxed mindset in themselves and
others that arises from foregoing one-upmanship. In bringing
people into harmony in this way—including friends, lovers,
and communities—bicycles are a great leveler. Whether
you're JFK or John Doe, you come as you are on a bike, and
the joys of cycling are the same.

And, as the saying goes, anyone can ride a bike. Cycling's
reputation for inclusivity was entrenched right from the start.
In the nineteenth century, women were subject to male

control and treated as second-class citizens. Many were confined to their homes or workplaces and forced to wear smothering clothes, such as heavy skirts, tight corsets, and restrictive collars. When bicycles came along, women were literally emancipated—through being able to travel much farther, choose whose company to keep, and wear liberal outfits more suited to cycling. Despite absurd rearguard warnings from pompous men claiming that bikes posed a threat to women's chastity and even fertility, the rise of cycling coincided with, and abetted, the rise of feminism. Today, thanks to the pioneering successes of this movement, we live in a more enlightened world—although many women still cherish the freedom that comes with cycling.

◆

Let me tell you what I think of bicycling.

I think it has done more to emancipate women

than anything else in the world.

SUSAN B. ANTHONY (1820–1906)
LEADING AMERICAN CAMPAIGNER, IN A "NEW YORK WORLD" INTERVIEW, 1896

◆

All Cyclists Great & Small

Cycling's inclusivity extends to children. On a bike, they can get to and from school, broaden their horizons, and shake off that protective layer their parents have wrapped them in. Even better, kids love it when adults join them on a bike ride. There are few more enjoyable family experiences.

The pleasures of cycling
are accessible to all.

At the other end of the scale are "silver" cyclists—those inspirational senior citizens who demonstrate that you're never too old to ride a bike, or even to learn how. Many of the core benefits of cycling are especially helpful to older people: independence, social interaction, mental stimulation, affordability, good health. And because you can exercise gently on a bike, or even choose a model that supplements your efforts with an electric motor, you can keep fit within your limits.

The same goes for overweight people. Cycling is a highly accessible form of exercise, much more so than jogging, which can be murder on the knees. Proportional to its own weight, a bicycle is capable of bearing a bigger load than an automobile, airplane, or bridge.

Even severe disabilities don't preclude cycling. Balancing on a bicycle may not be possible for everybody, but there are different kinds of cycles to accommodate different user needs. There are hand-powered cycles for people who can't use their legs; four-wheelers with back support for people who need extra stability; side-by-side bikes or tandems for people who need a carer next to them; there are even cycles designed to carry wheelchairs. The pleasures of cycling are accessible to all.

Emmeline's Ascent

Back when her kind should've kept
the fact of ankles to themselves,
it was mildly surprising:
that from the ground—where her
neat boots were tied with satin bows
and her knees, unremarked-on, stood
fixed beneath a triple skirt and had not
one single scar to boast of—she
thought to ascend the small stepladder
borrowed for the job from someone's father
and, loosely grasping the hand of a stranger,
swing brilliantly from the hip one long
athletic leg over the rim, into unsupported
territory, without even a pale second
given over to the fear of falling the five
shameful feet back to zero, from such
a high wheel; and that once up there
she recognized herself seeing not what
she never before could've imagined,
but everything exactly as it was—the
clear hard road, made for going along;
the terraces lined up for her admiration;
and on the other side of the clipped hedge
the unhatted men in the park, a few streets
but miles asunder from closed offices,
airing the first hint of their balding crowns
to the pigeons and anyone else geared up
for once to peer down on them from above.

REBECCA WATTS

COMMUNITY SPIRITED

◆

On a bike, you get closer to your local environment, and being out and about in the community brings a feeling of belonging. You discover you don't need to go back in time to enjoy these nostalgic experiences. Yet bicycles don't just make local life more pleasant for cyclists—they make it more pleasant for everyone.

CYCLING'S CONTRIBUTION TO AIR AND NOISE POLLUTION is zero. Bicycles hardly ever cause harm to other road users in collisions. And cyclists help raise "social capital," the extent to which local people are bonded together. Higher social capital has many profound and useful effects, including reducing crime and mental illness, and making communities happier, healthier, richer, and more egalitarian.

Compare this to the effects of cars on local life. They emit toxic fumes, which cause medical problems, such as asthma and even cancer. They generate noise, which creates disturbance at night and stress during the day. They inflict countless injuries and fatalities upon pedestrians, cyclists, and other car users. And they lower social capital by segregating drivers or passengers and their fellow citizens.

Yet bikes are woefully underused. Obviously, you can't always cycle—some journeys are too long, some loads are too heavy. But even when it comes to short, unencumbered trips, the likes of which are especially common in cities, many car drivers continue to shun the bicycle. In the United States, a vast country in which long car journeys are par for the course, almost one-third of the gasoline pumped from service stations fuels trips of three miles or less.

It's not even as if these short trips benefit the drivers. In trying to gain an advantage, they actually all end up worse off—stuck in congestion. The futility of a traffic jam is similar to the futility of trying to keep up with the Joneses. When people buy fancy possessions or clothes, trying to outdo each other, they all end up looking the same, and worse off, having wasted their money.

Do unto Others …

In opting out of these futile arms races, cyclists come out better off. Unfortunately, they still have to suffer (arguably more than anyone) the impact of cars on communities, but many cyclists are consoled by the fact that they gain something much deeper than convenience or affordability: they gain moral values.

After all, morality's core principle—often called the "golden rule"—tells us to treat others as we want to be treated, and on a bike we tend to do so. Most cyclists don't want to experience congestion, pollution, danger, and an antisocial atmosphere, so they refrain from contributing to these things. Most cyclists don't wish to be goaded by flashy status symbols, so they refrain from buying them.

Cycling is an example of an activity in which what's best for the community is best for individuals too. In other words, values can make everyone better off. In the happiest communities, each person looks out for each other, or for the whole group, and from this everyone benefits. Indeed, our brains are hardwired to achieve this effect; neuroscientists have found that when people perform good deeds, they experience a pleasurable sensation. It seems that if you want to feel good, you need to be good. And cycling is a good place to start.

GETTING A JOB

If I had a penny for every time someone has said "get a job" to me, I would never need to work again. For a while, I didn't have to. As a philosopher, I spent a decade opting out of society. I felt I had more important problems to worry about. How do I know what's true? Why is my pain mine? Am I free? Why am I always here now? It was highly introspective stuff. Even when I did take the time to think about other people, there was an element of philosophy's characteristic egocentricity involved. How do I know the right thing to do? Can I trust what people say? Do other people have minds like mine?

I GRADUALLY CAME TO REALIZE that philosophical navel-gazing goes hand in hand with a peculiarly anxious attitude to other people. I began to wonder whether the general parody of philosophers—work-shy, hypochondriac loners—might be onto something. Could it be that my attitude to society explained my interest in philosophical problems, instead of my interest in philosophy explaining my attitude to society?

Recovering from Philosophy

This, I figured, might be the reason such problems are so stubbornly insoluble. Maybe they are a smoke screen. Maybe philosophers invent these problems to avoid facing up to society. Obviously, these thoughts weren't popular with my colleagues, but by now I didn't care. I was more interested in what was happening in the rest of society. I was recovering from philosophy.

I'm still recovering from philosophy. Sometimes when I feel myself drifting into excessive introspection, cycling reminds me of where I belong. Instead of worrying about my connections to other people, as philosophers tend to do, I go out and experience my neighborhood. I move with the traffic; I slot into a working community; I look into people's eyes; I turn strangers into acquaintances. I am mindful of others.

Sometimes when I feel myself drifting into excessive introspection, cycling reminds me of where I belong.

CHAPTER FOUR

$$E = mc^2$$

AROUND THE WORLD

Cycling promotes a "global" attitude just like
Einstein's. In embarking on and reflecting on long-
distance cycle rides, we can extend our horizons and
limits—whether through racing or roaming, we see the
world from a new perspective. We get closer to nature,
yet perceive its awesome scale and profound beauty.
And, far from home, we find common ground with
other cultures; we learn the value of international
cooperation. We become mindful of humanity.

MORE IMPORTANT STARS

◆

The universe created us, yet we act as though we are separate from it. Einstein described this sense of detachment as a "delusion" that imprisons our hearts and minds. "Our task," he claimed, "must be to free ourselves from the prison by widening our circle of compassion to embrace all living creatures and the whole of nature in its beauty."

WHEN IT COMES TO EXPANSIVE THINKING, few are better qualified than Albert Einstein. In physics his theories tracked the unimaginably small and the unfathomably big. Delving into matter, he encountered an invisible ocean teeming with molecules, atoms, and electrons yet swathed in emptiness. Looking out from the world, he saw this pattern projected—hundreds of billions of galaxies separated by expanding deserts of space, a strewn universe racing away from itself in all directions. And, of course, Einstein appreciated the biggest marvel of all: that the human intellect can travel to such extremes.

Like all great voyagers, Einstein found consolation in the openness laid out before him. "We must remember that this is a very small star," he once remarked of humanity's troubled neighborhood, "and probably some of the larger and more important stars may be very virtuous and happy."

Bird of Passage

Earth is even smaller than the particularly small star around which it orbits, yet our planet is plenty big enough for countless lifetimes of exploration. Einstein, a self-styled "bird of passage," made the most of his opportunity. He first developed itinerant habits as a youth, when he would take bike tours with his friends. As an aspiring scientist, he saw such excursions as a time to contemplate the world. They were also a chance for him to bond with his favorite peer, Mileva Marić. While daydreaming about their future together, he wrote to her: "No matter what happens, we'll have the most wonderful life in the world ... we can buy bicycles and take a bike tour every couple of weeks."

Einstein's propensity to keep moving characterized his professional life. His career included positions at seven different research institutions—a good haul, considering how long it took him to get his first academic job. Not one to do things by halves, when changing jobs meant changing countries, Einstein often switched nationalities. In his lifetime, he was German, Swiss, Austrian, German again, then American. He was even stateless for a while, the first time he left his place of birth.

Roving Star

Einstein's successes as a physicist coincided with the first age of global celebrity. The early twentieth century was a time of great economic expansion, when automobiles added to the reach of shipping, railroads, and bicycles, while the development of radio supplemented existing communications, such as newspapers and telegrams. In this burgeoning web of connectedness, news traveled ever faster, and the most outstanding events and individuals found a global audience. Einstein's theoretical breakthroughs fitted the bill, as did his wacky, endearing appearance and witty quotability. He wasn't the dreary nerd that people expected; they were enthralled.

As Einstein's fame expanded, so did his wandering. His visits became lucrative official tours, taking in numerous countries, including France, England, Japan, Israel, Brazil, Cuba, Panama, Palestine, and Australia. Crowds gathered in the streets to greet him, and his lectures captivated packed auditoriums, even when he spoke in German. He rubbed shoulders with the rich, powerful, and famous. He was offered movie roles—and the presidency of Israel. Both he declined.

Yet Einstein's sense of his own Jewishness grew throughout his life. He was well aware that his wandering was in part involuntary, in a turbulent era that saw European Jews scattered across the globe. He used his fame to raise money for good causes, including that of the persecuted Jewish people.

One World

In effortlessly communing with his hosts wherever he went, Einstein became convinced that, despite superficial cultural differences, people everywhere belong to one human race.

He saw that all human beings have the same basic body form and biological requirements, such as food and water. He also saw that all human beings share mental and emotional characteristics: common hopes, desires, needs, pleasures, sorrows, and so on. These observations heightened and broadened Einstein's sense of empathy. He felt a kinship with all of humanity, and became a self-styled "citizen of the world."

The Great Goal

Einstein's enlightened outlook intensified his anguish at the turmoil and bloodshed he witnessed during his lifetime. In two global conflagrations, and in between, the world's societies were united, above all else, in mutual enmity. Einstein drew the logical conclusion: That human nature must contain some seed that can grow into bigotry and war.

Yet Einstein was no pessimist. He didn't think fighting was inevitable. Instead, he wrote of "his devotion to the great goal of the internal and external liberation of man from the evils of war." He knew that human nature manifests itself in different ways, depending on the circumstances, and that the task of civilization is to discover the best way to promote moral behavior and demote wrongdoing. In a swipe at relativists of the day, who were hiding from the complexities of the real world, he offered words of praise for the psychologist Sigmund Freud: "Your sense of reality is less clouded by wishful thinking."

World Unity

Einstein ardently believed that international cooperation is the only way to achieve peace. Carrying his aversion to nationalism to its logical end point, he envisaged a world government with a monopoly on the use of force, thereby empowered to arbitrate in international squabbles or intervene whenever national governments oppress their own citizens. In effect, Einstein argued that the whole world should become a federation of states, united by the universal principles of democracy and peaceful coexistence.

◆

The only salvation for civilization and the
human race lies in the creation of a world government.

EINSTEIN

◆

As he did in physics, in world affairs Einstein sought unity. When his own scientific theories inspired the development of nuclear weapons, his ardor for peace grew—influenced, perhaps, by a measure of unwarranted guilt (it was his letter that tipped off the American government about the theoretical possibility of a nuclear detonation; but, from that point on, Einstein had no personal involvement in the "Manhattan Project" which built the first atomic bomb). He went on to chair an organization demanding nuclear arms control through world government. The stakes, he felt, were too high for a responsible intellectual to do otherwise.

◆

The unleashed power of the atom has changed

everything save our modes of thinking.

EINSTEIN

◆

A Deeply Religious Nonbeliever

Awestruck by the sprawling beauty of the universe, and the exquisite rationality of its laws, Einstein concluded that reality itself is equivalent to God. But he didn't believe in what he called a "personal" God, a ghostly despot who is interested in human affairs, answers prayers, appreciates rituals, welcomes some people to heaven, punishes others in hell, and has a plan for the universe. Einstein saw this kind of religion as naive and divisive. He insisted that "the path to genuine religiosity does not lie through the fear of life, and the fear of death, and blind faith, but through striving after rational knowledge." In other words, Einstein claimed, the only way to know God is through knowing the world better.

This claim amounted to a vision of unity of the most profound kind—between science and religion, and among religions (if the universe is God, there is only one God). Einstein was reaching out a hand of reconciliation and urging all religions to do the same. If a scientist could appreciate that the universe is Godlike, then perhaps religious believers could countenance the idea that God is equivalent to the impersonal universe described by science. Alas, Einstein's subtlety was met with scorn by many leading religious figures. In their eyes, to be a "deeply religious nonbeliever," as he called himself, was still to be a nonbeliever.

When faced with intransigence, Einstein consoled himself with characteristic wit: "Two things are infinite: the universe and human stupidity; and I'm not sure about the universe."

NEW HORIZONS

I live in a town of giants. They pace down streets, and from one to the other, with scarcely a thought for town planning, while little people scurry around below, or race alongside in metal cages. The giants just smile, and go gently. Whenever the swarm grows tiresome, they step out into the countryside, alone or together, to gambol down quiet lanes and across meadows. Giants relish open space. Some tread continents to find it—over mist-veiled mountains and unchanging deserts, where even giants grow weary. They soon seek the comfort of humanity once again. And they find it—wherever they are. From a broad perspective, humanity is one.

WITH THE INVENTION OF THE BICYCLE, legwork could carry people farther than ever before. It was as though cycling had turned its practitioners into giants—more than a match for the horses that had abetted human mobility for millennia. When the first human-iron hybrids nonchalantly passed by, onlookers must have been stunned, and not a little alarmed. Perhaps the spectacle would have been similar to the modern-day experience of seeing someone walking mysteriously quickly on a horizontal escalator, although the dreamlike bafflement of watching a pioneer cyclist gliding by would have been longer-lasting.

But not indefinite. The affordability of bicycles meant that they caught on quickly, and soon giants were proliferating at all levels of society. In cities, workers abandoned crowded tenement buildings and headed for the suburbs, because longer commutes were now possible. In the countryside, the gene pool widened, as distant towns suddenly became more readily accessible. As people's horizons expanded, the question about cycling became not how, but how far and how fast?

Farther, Faster

Long-distance cyclists experience everything that's great about cycling, but to an extreme degree. Whereas most of us rarely stray more than a few miles from civilization, and push ourselves only a little, endurance cycling is about pushing beyond all known limits: of the body, of the bike, of mental fortitude. Right from the start, cycling's history charts a spectacular expansion of the possible. Reflecting on this amazing story adds inspiration to a regular cycle ride.

Speeds attained and distances covered on a bike are all the more impressive when the achievements are combined. In the early days of the pedal bicycle, this was especially apparent.

After all, trudging a long way slowly and scampering a short trip quickly were mundane facts of human locomotion—it was traveling far and fast without the aid of horses that was the stuff of fantasy.

The Best of British

Britain was an early hotbed of such marvelous feats. In July 1869, the press reported that R. J. Klamroth had ridden from London to Edinburgh, covering 400 miles in six days. In total, he was on his bike for sixty-five hours, with an average speed of seven-and-a-half miles per hour. He enjoyed a good sleep each night, napped in the afternoons, and swigged sherry while in the saddle. The public were delighted. Other heroes that year included John Henry Palmer, who took just three days to cycle 220 miles from Newcastle-on-Tyne to his home in Birmingham, and three friends—Charles Spencer, Rowley Turner, and John Mayall—who rode 55 miles from London to Brighton in a day. Mayall arrived first, in twelve hours, and promptly hit the town.

In the months and years that followed, such feats of endurance became both commonplace and more striking. There was the Scotsman who, in a single day in 1869, pedaled a rugged 83 miles from his home near Glasgow to Oban. There were three members of the Amateur Bicycle Club in England who, in 1871, rode 100 miles in a day, stopping only to wheel triumphantly among the pillars of Stonehenge.

Two years later, four enthusiasts from the same club needed just two weeks to complete 700 miles from London to John O'Groats, the most northeasterly point in Scotland. And better was to come. In 1891 Keith-Falconer was able to reach the same destination starting from Land's End, the most southwesterly place in Britain, covering nearly 1,000 miles in just thirteen days. A year later, J. W. F. Sutton cycled an astonishing 260 miles in under twenty-four hours.

The scene was set for one of the greatest heroines of the women's liberation movement. In 1893, sixteen-year-old Tessie Reynolds rode from her home in Brighton to London and back again, in a single day. She was daringly dressed—in an open jacket and pants cropped below the knee. Her accomplishment spoke of equality in both rights and abilities.

Across Continents

All over the world, cyclists impressed. In 1875, a Frenchman rode 700 miles to Vienna in twelve days. In 1890, a Russian lieutenant rode 2,000 miles from St. Petersburg to London, arriving in a month. Not to be outdone, in 1896 an American lieutenant cycled with twenty Buffalo Soldiers—black army volunteers—2,000 miles from Montana to St Louis.

Even when motorcycles became available, pedal bikes continued to grab headlines. In 1899, Charles "Mile-a-Minute" Murphy kept pace with an express train on a three-mile stretch of the Long Island Rail Road. During the second mile, he reached a speed of 60 mph—equal to the fastest motor-cycles of the day. At the other end of the scale were the distance-devouring bicycle messengers of the early twentieth century. In 1915, John Dixon from Dallas pedaled 16,000 miles in six months, in the course of carrying out his daily deliveries. He was paid by the mile.

Six-Day Races

In cycling's pioneering days, pushing the boundaries of speed and distance rapidly became an organized pursuit. On the road, impressive competitive achievements racked up, but it was on the smoother surfaces of specially created circular cycling tracks—indoor or outdoor "velodromes"—where the most jaw-dropping performances took place. In 1874, after the press had ridiculed David Stanton's claim that he had ridden from Bath to London in only eight-and-a-half hours, he repeated the feat publicly on an indoor track, completing 100 miles in less than eight hours.

And he wasn't done yet. A year later Stanton wowed crowds by completing 650 track miles in seven successive days. It was a wildly popular achievement, so the format was carried forward, minus the Sunday. These endurance events became known as "six-day races" and were staged the world over—the idea being, simply, for competitors to ride as far as they could in six days. During one such event in 1878, Stanton managed a distance of more than 1,000 miles.

Enduring Appeal

The six-day race format remains popular today, but two endurance events have endured above all. In 1891, Frenchman Pierre Giffard organized a long-distance cycle race to promote the Parisian newspaper he was editing, *Le Petit Journal*. The route stretched from Paris to the coastal town of Brest at the end of the Breton peninsula in northwest France, before turning around and ending back in the capital. There were 207 participants, ninety-nine of whom completed the 800-mile course. The winner, Charles Terrant, crossed the line in just 71 hours and 22 minutes.

It was ten years before the second Paris-Brest-Paris race took place, such was the logistical complexity of organizing it. This once-a-decade schedule remained in place for six races, culminating in the 1951 event won by Maurice Diot, in a time of 38 hours and 55 minutes, which remains the course record (partly because the route has since been shifted around repeatedly, becoming notably more hilly).

Today, the Paris-Brest-Paris ride takes place every four years. The most significant change, however, is that the event's competitive element is now restricted to a small group of racers who set off separately from the rest of the field. Everyone else rides with the sole aim of completing the course, which they must do within bounds set by upper and lower average speed limits. This more leisurely format is known as a "randonée." There are numerous such events staged throughout the world, typically covering distances of between 50 and 1,000 miles. A randoneur rides for glory (or charity) without necessarily racing.

A Famous Race

There is, however, one particular time-honored cycling event that remains utterly a race. And while it may not quite be the oldest, it is the most famous. In 1901, daily newspaper *Le Vélo* cosponsored the Paris-Brest-Paris event, a move that led to excellent sales. A rival paper, *L'Auto-Velo*, picked up the scent and, persuaded by their visionary cycling editor Georges Lefevre, decided to host their own cycle race in 1903. The course covered 1,500 miles over eighteen days, starting in Paris and passing through Lyon, Marseille, Toulouse, Bordeaux, and Nantes before returning to the capital. Sixty racers were on the start line; twenty made it to the finish. The event may have struggled to attract riders, but it was popular with the public. With crowds lining the route, and Parisians turning out en masse to watch winner Maurice Garin cross the line in 95.5 hours, the Tour de France was here to stay.

Today, the annual Tour spans twenty-one days in a series of separate stages and covers about 2,200 miles. Over the years, the route has varied, ranging from 1,509 to 3,570 miles, and taking in numerous regions and even countries. Mountainous stages have increased the agony and awe. The famous yellow jersey, worn by the race leader, has added to the drama.

◆

There simply is nothing else like it …

It's the only race in the world where you have to get

a haircut halfway through.

CHRIS BOARDMAN (1968–)
BRITISH OLYMPIC CYCLING GOLD MEDALIST

◆

A Grueling Challenge

Tour racers typically burn 6,000–10,000 calories a day, riding an average speed of 24 mph for 125 miles a day (with only two rest days), and scaling the equivalent of three Mount Everests. The challenge, surely one of the most arduous in all of sport, has spawned many legends, such as Jacques Anquetil (between 1957 and 1964), Eddy Merckx (between 1969 and 1975), Bernard Hinault (between 1978 and 1985), and Miguel Indurain (between 1991 and 1995), each of whom won five titles. My favourite winner is Sir Bradley Wiggins, who in 2012 became the first Briton to lift the trophy, and was promptly knighted by the Queen. With his bushy sideburns, down-to-earth personality, and clean sporting reputation, Wiggins became a hero to wannabe sports champions the world over.

The Tour de France is one of three similar "grand tours" in Europe, along with the Giro d'Italia (Tour of Italy), established in 1909, and the Vuelta a España (Tour of Spain), established in 1935. In the United States, however, an even bigger challenge has grown in popularity in recent decades, attesting to the continuing allure of pushing the boundaries in long-distance cycling. In 1982, the first Race Across America took place, a 3,000 mile-long slog from Santa Monica to the Empire State Building. Founder John Marino was joined by just three other competitors, all of whom beat him. Winner Lon Haldeman completed the course in under ten days.

The race has since been held annually, with a route that has varied while always measuring a few hundred miles either side of the original total distance, and always heading from west to east, coast to coast. There are now several hundred entrants each year, who cover 250–350 miles in a day, staying on the bike even when nature calls, and sleeping for just two or three hours a night. This is probably the only sporting event in the world where hallucinations are a documented hazard. It is definitely the only sporting event where any competitor has complained of being attacked by monstrous trees, chased by howling bearded men, or threatened by mailboxes.

All the Way

The ultimate achievement in long-distance cycling is to circumnavigate the globe. By now, you're probably suspecting that humanity hasn't shied away from this challenge—and you'd be right. People have been cycling around the world for almost as long as cycling has been around. The first such epic journey was accomplished by Englishman Thomas Stevens. Starting out in April 1884 in San Francisco, he rode east, across the United States, Europe, and Asia, before arriving back where he began, nearly three years, several boat journeys, and 13,500 pedaled miles later.

The history of cycling is peppered with many such successes, but most took place before 2005, when a new formal definition of a round-the-world bicycle journey was agreed. To officially meet the criteria, a cyclist must now pass through two opposite points on the surface of the globe, and complete a journey of a minimum of 24,900 miles (equal to the length of the equator), of which at least 18,000 must be cycled.

Record Breakers

Perhaps cajoled into competition by this unambiguous framework, in the last decade a series of adventurers have smashed the round-the-world cycling record. Steve Strange completed the journey in 276 days. Mark Beaumont followed up with 194 days. James Bowthorpe managed it in 175. Julian Sayarer made it in 169. Vincent Cox did it in 163. And then came a quantum leap: Alan Bate in 106 days. His trip was the first to be accompanied by a support team, which partly explains his astonishing performance. But he still had to pedal. His topsy-turvy route began in Bangkok, passed through Australia and New Zealand, veered up into San Francisco, continued on to Halifax in Canada, detoured down to lower South America, moved up to Brazil, crossed over to Western Europe, headed into Great Britain via France, swung down toward

Italy, passed through Greece, carried on into the Middle East and East Asia, and finished back in Bangkok.

No doubt, the record will keep falling. I'll bet you, one day someone will cycle around the world in eighty days.

More Gain Than Pain

Long-distance cycling comes with many potential hardships. There's the physical discomfort: the blistered groin, bad back, neck pain, sore wrists, numb hands, knee problems, earaches, dust-filled eyes, stomach cramps, nausea, infectious diseases, athlete's foot, sunburn, dehydration, altitude sickness, nosebleeds, and the scream of lactic acid in the muscles. There's the mental toll: the drowsiness, dizziness, loneliness (or its opposite, irritation caused by ever-present accompanying riders), homesickness, and the disorientation of sleeping in a new place every night. There are the hazards: bicycle malfunction, poor surfaces (gravelly, uneven, melted, slippery, or filled with potholes), extreme weather (hot, cold, snowy, rainy, windy, stormy, and foggy), stray animals in the road (dogs, sheep, cows, horses, and even swarms of frogs), dangerous wildlife (snakes, bears, insects, and spiders), and unpredictable terrain (many remote areas of the world are still uncharted, or change too quickly to be charted).

Worst of all, there's the dreaded "bonk," also known as "hitting the wall"—when your body is so energy-depleted you just can't go on.

And, believe it or not, people do it for fun! A long-distance ride completed for no reason other than enjoyment is called a "tour" (despite, confusingly, some races calling themselves tours). On a tour you can make up your own itinerary—no course, no competition, no clock. Are cycle tourists crazy to pedal hundreds or thousands of miles without a specific reason? Not at all. For one thing, the hardships of long-distance cycling are much less severe when you adopt a more leisurely pace and relax, instead of pursuing records, chasing other riders, or meeting epic route requirements. But, most importantly, the benefits of long-distance cycling accrue much more easily and lastingly when you do it for fun.

Ride with a View

Touring involves a lot of pedaling, but that's not the most breathtaking aspect of the experience. One of the greatest pleasures of seeing the world by bike is encountering its stunning natural beauty: chirping meadows, secluded bays, roaring waterfalls, wild deserts, rolling hills, shimmering lakes, quiet valleys, snow-capped peaks, rocky streams, gliding rivers, serene flatlands, vast skies, redolent forests, rugged cliffs, and blankets of flowers.

Cycle touring doesn't just present you with such experiences—it magnifies them. This is partly because cycling brings you into direct contact with your surroundings and heightens your attention, which makes all the details in a

MINDFULNESS OF BODY

✳

Naturally, cycle touring is less demanding than racing. This means that you're less likely to experience hardships on tour; but it also means that, if you do, you can afford to relax and adopt a more mindful attitude toward them. In particular, practicing a "mindfulness of body" meditation can help you to come to terms with any aches and pains you develop during a long ride.

Take a break, and just focus on your breathing. But this time allow your attention to migrate throughout your whole body. You could try consciously "moving" your awareness gently downward; passing it slowly into your neck, shoulders, chest, stomach, sides, pelvis, groin, thighs, knees, shins, feet, and toes. Then back again if you want.

As your attention wanders, just notice any bodily sensations you experience. Pleasant feelings, neutral feelings, or feelings of tiredness, soreness, and pain—try not to judge them as good or bad. Just be curious about them. Imagine you are observing a novel pattern or an unusual color, as though you've never experienced such a sensation and are intrigued.

If you have any thoughts about what you're experiencing, then let them go, like clouds. Just *be* with your body. In becoming more comfortable with it, you may find that your body feels more comfortable.

scene burst out in slow motion. But it's also because cycle touring comes with an enhanced sense of scale. When you go, you go with a load that's as light as possible, for reasons of speed as well as storage limitation. You carry just a few essentials, such as spare clothing, a tool kit, a tent, food, and water, foregoing many of the luxuries of modern life. In doing so, you are reminded of your place in the order of things, beyond the magnolia walls of home. You see the true vastness of nature and its uncompromising grandeur.

In waking up from the anesthesia of everyday life, it's not uncommon for cycle tourists to experience a feeling that the world is more profound than they realized; that hidden depths and complexities abound. It's as if riders uncover a priceless painting beneath a grubby exterior, polish up a pebble to reveal a diamond, or open up a dusty box to be greeted by charming music. You don't have to belong to a religion to experience this sense of amazement that reality resonates, sparkles, and sings so beautifully. If anything, the experience transplants the heart of religion into the here and now. Instead of going to heaven to find the world's hidden glory, you can find it on a bicycle.

Humanity

It's not just natural scenes that look more beautiful from a bike. Due to your heightened sensory awareness and exposure to the physical environment, man-made landscapes and structures seem more impressive, too: awesome bridges, weathered lighthouses, gleaming cityscapes, imposing castles, majestic temples, pretty towns, grand monuments, and highways stretching to the horizon. All these shine out as what they are—great feats of design, engineering, and labor.

When touring, your relationship to the people you meet along the way is similarly enhanced. Unscreened, you encounter far-flung communities alertly and sensitively, in the same way as you experience your own community when cycling. And your unencumbered state amplifies your sense of communion with the people around you.

When you pedal into a town or city, you are likely to be highly aware of your dependence on the people there. After hours, days, weeks, or months in the saddle, you may need food or water. You may need shelter from bad weather, a place to sleep, or just directions and some local knowledge. You may need to repair your bicycle, perhaps through acquiring tools or parts, or having it dealt with by a local tradesperson. Or you might just want companionship—someone to talk to, a crowd to melt into, or a dance floor to stagger onto.

Start with a Smile ...
Many of these requirements subtly influence your attitude to your hosts. As well as viewing their cultural particularities as curiosities, you feel the need to make a deeper connection. You start with a smile—the gesture of disarmament innate to all human beings. You then seek to establish other such

similarities, to understand who you are dealing with—what are their motivations and their potentialities for you. You try to get into their heads, so as to benefit from what's inside.

In this way, whenever you meet new people, including fellow travelers, you discover a zone of mutual understanding that lies beyond any superficial differences between you. It's a comforting feeling, but it's as profound as any encounter with natural or artificial splendor. When you tour, you automatically make the effort to peer beneath the convoluted surface of culture, and there you find humanity.

A United World

The history of the human race is, above all, a story of integration. As raindrops collect to form puddles that merge into pools, smaller groups of people have amalgamated into larger societies, and those into larger ones still. Starting out as motley bands of hunter-gatherers roaming grasslands and occasionally meeting neighboring groups, the human species has gradually metamorphosed into a global community.

This increasing integration has been made possible by four interrelated forces. Improvements in communication, from the alphabet to the Internet, have yielded greater mutual understanding. Advances in travel, from the horse to the airplane, have enabled people to journey farther and faster. The expansion of trade across continents has brought increasing mutual gains, aided by the invention of money, which has

CYCLING & DEVELOPMENT

✽

In the West, we have outgrown the bicycle as our main means of economic development. With planes, trains, and automobiles fulfilling our long-distance transportation requirements, we tend to use bikes for shorter journeys or recreation.

In the developing world, things are different. Bicycles remain a vital form of transportation over both long and short distances, for ferrying goods or people. In many places, even ambulances are pedaled, exemplifying how the mobility afforded by cycling can literally be a matter of life and death.

In far-flung developing communities, pedaling is also used as a source of power. You can pedal to husk corn, sharpen a knife, charge a battery, filter water, pump water (or a latrine), cross a river, or wash clothes. Remember all this, when you next set out on your beloved bicycle. Pedaling would mean even more to you if you lived in the developing world.

---

enabled complex exchanges to take place. The growth of governance has provided the legal and physical infrastructure— laws and roads—to give direction to human progress.

The world today is far from perfect, and is full of inequalities both within and between nations, but, on the whole, integration brings with it greater wealth, better health, longer lives, lower infant mortality, more democracy, less prejudice, and dramatically reduced levels of violence, including wars.

These benefits have accrued spectacularly during the second half of the twentieth century and into the twenty-first, in a time of accelerating global integration. It turns out that Einstein's instincts were right. We don't quite have a world government, but the globalization of communication, travel, and trade has coincided with a profusion of international organizations and pacts, such as the United Nations and the Nuclear Non-Proliferation Treaty. The outcome has been a relatively conflict-free period now known as "the long peace," one unprecedented in human history.

These gains, however, haven't been entirely painless. Globalization has brought with it a pace of life many find intolerably fast, and an upheaval of cherished traditions and social structures. With the expansion of trade, everything seems to have a price on it. Governments are unwieldy yet pedantic. Our tranquility gets punctured by an intrusive media. Everyone seems to be constantly on the move.

It's easy to lose sight of the bigger picture—how lucky we are to live in a time of such peace, prosperity, and opportunity as this global era has afforded us. Even when we travel far, our horizons are seldom genuinely broadened. Long-haul flights dull our senses. In new places, our encounters are sanitized by comfortable hotels, credit cards, and inauthentic pandering hosts. We derive no sense of the profound importance of communing with other cultures, so when faced with the downsides of globalization, we become complacent about its benefits.

Traveling Mindfully

On a bicycle tour, we travel mindfully, and our horizons, like those of the early bicycle pioneers, are genuinely expanded. Propelled by our own hard work, we truly appreciate the marvel of long-distance travel. We experience the vastness of the globe, and get a more accurate sense of the myriad opportunities that are out there. In distancing ourselves from the comforts of our everyday lives, we come to realize how incredible the achievements of civilization are. In communing more authentically with far-flung cultures, we perceive the value of global cooperation firsthand. And, like all cycling-inspired epiphanies, these effects endure long after the ride is over. We come to feel more at home in an integrated world.

My First Long-Distance Ride

It once seemed inconceivable to me that I could ride more than a few miles in a day. Everyone I knew thought that cycling around the block was some kind of extreme sport. The idea of long-distance cycling struck us all as madness.

Then, at university, I met a mathematician who, characteristically, had thought about it more logically. You can easily walk ten miles in a day, so you can easily cycle 50. I learned this while he was passing through Cambridge (where I now live, in England), on his way to Edinburgh. He had started off in Portsmouth, on the south coast of England, and planned to make the trip in under a week. When he rolled up at my house, I couldn't quite believe how far he'd already come in a day. (I was more convinced once he had eaten almost everything in my cupboards.) Four days later, I received a text message saying he had made it all the way to Scotland.

Inspired by his nonchalant heroism, I decided I would cycle back to Cambridge the next time I was visiting London, more than 50 miles away. When the day came, it was lovely and sunny, and in no time I was halfway home, passing by cabbage fields and quaint old farmhouses. I stopped to have lunch—cheese sandwiches—under a little tree beside the road. I felt perhaps the most contented I ever have. It wasn't a complicated feeling—just a sense of pride that I had got so far by my own efforts. In that beautiful countryside, surrounded by a whole different way of life, I felt I'd come a million miles.

Ten miles south of Cambridge, I made a last stop, at a gasoline station. I asked the attendant if I could refill my water bottle. She filled it for me instead of trying to sell me a drink. I think she was impressed by my journey. Three-and-a-half hours after I started, I arrived in Cambridge.

With an unbroken string of memories trailing behind me, connecting every vivid stage of my journey, it was all the more exhilarating to breathe the air of another city. I suddenly appreciated for the first time in my life what distance really is. It's not time spent waiting to arrive somewhere. It's space, vast and overflowing with experiences. I texted my friend: "The eagle has landed." I couldn't wait to fly again.

$$E = {}_m c^2$$

A BALANCED LIFE

*As a living meditation,
cycling encourages a holistic
philosophy just like Einstein's. On a
bike, we cultivate practical, individual, local,
and global attitudes, which enhance each other
through their combination. At the end of our journey,
we have an opportunity to reflect on where we've been
and to carry our experiences forward. In turn, our
enlightened outlook lifts us, bringing us renewed
calm and happiness. Through mastering the
art of mindful cycling, we achieve balance
in the modern world.*

JOURNEY'S END

◆

On April 12, 1955, Einstein went to his Princeton office to work. He had a pain in his groin, and it showed on his face. His assistant asked if everything was alright. "Yes it is," Einstein smiled, "but I am not." The next day, he collapsed. An aneurysm on his abdominal aorta, diagnosed years earlier, had started to rupture. A group of doctors convened in his house and recommended a surgeon who might be able to operate, albeit not likely successfully. Einstein refused: "I've done my share. It's time to go." The next morning, he woke in agony and was rushed to hospital, where he rallied for a few days, scribbling pages of equations and working on a speech for an engagement he would never fulfill: "I stand before you today not as an American citizen and not as a Jew, but as a human being." At 1:00 a.m. on April 18, a nurse heard him shouting something in German, and rushed to his bedside. Albert Einstein was dead. He was cremated that same day, in a modest ceremony attended, according to his wishes, by just twelve people. Einstein died as he lived—a willful individual, a devoted scientist, a committed internationalist, a humble soul.

W HEN YOU LOOK BACK OVER YOUR LIFE, what kind of person do you want to see? Someone who lived as fully as Einstein? Someone who valued science, technology, and reality, who championed creativity, determination, and audacity, who cherished humility, modesty, and neighborliness, and who appreciated humanity's bigger picture?

He remained sane in a mad world.

BERTRAND RUSSELL (1872–1970)
PHILOSOPHER, DESCRIBING ALBERT EINSTEIN

The most inspirational thing about Einstein is that he manifested each of these attitudes to an amazing degree: he was brilliantly practical; he exuded individuality in everything he did; his local ways were exceptionally endearing; his internationalism was unflagging. You'd assume that a jack-of-all mindsets would be master of none—that you can't combine practical, individual, local, and global attitudes without each one being compromised. But Einstein's life reveals the contrary—that together these four attitudes are enhanced.

Most of us take a different approach. We cultivate one of these attitudes, while excluding, or even denigrating, the others. We act as though our brains were lopsided, biased toward the left, right, back, or front, where, respectively, the practical, individual, local, and global attitudes reside. (The same is true at the level of society, where our attitudes tend to sort us into mutually exclusive groups.) Sometimes we even become philosophers, worrying incessantly and pointlessly about life's conflicts and contrasts.

Modern life is stressful, and when we become stressed we become set in our ways. Caught up in our thoughts, sensations, and feelings, we persist obsessively, as though blinkered, with a particular attitude. The moral of Einstein's life is that we'd all be better off with a more balanced approach. Whatever our agendas, we'd feel more fulfilled if we adopted each of the four attitudes identified in this book, instead of just one, and allowed them all to enhance each other.

A Wonderful Blend

When you think about it, the synergies are obvious. Learning about reality enhances our creativity, while our imaginations help us develop greater practical awareness. An integrated global society enriches local life, while thriving communities contribute to a wider economy. A creative outlook makes us more expansive in our worldview, while traveling and embracing the world expands our imaginations. A practical mindset equips us to contribute to our local communities, while interacting with our neighbors helps us share useful skills. Global integration augments our technologies, while scientific developments facilitate globalization. Expressing ourselves through creativity instead of one-upmanship helps us see eye to eye with our neighbors, while friendly communities encourage us to express our individuality.

We can all achieve these positive ways of living through mindful meditation, a practice that enables us to avoid getting caught up in our thoughts, sensations, and feelings, allowing our whole worldview to recover a natural balance. But sometimes we're so busy that we can't find time to meditate, and, even when we do, we are so stressed that the long-term benefits are lost. We fall back into our lopsided habits.

A Living Meditation

Cycling is a living meditation: It allows us to achieve mindfulness not in a hidden retreat but in the full flow of life, while still deriving the same lasting benefits. Both on and off the bike, those four attitudes gather spontaneously around our paths, like clouds. We acquire practical understanding through learning how our bike works, preparing for each ride, and facing reality unscreened. We express our individuality by pedaling our way to greater freedom, creativity, and determination. We enhance our local sensibilities by getting to know our neighborhoods better and becoming more sociable. We develop a worldly outlook through experiencing firsthand the true meaning of distance, the unity of human nature, and the value of human integration.

Through cycling we keep our balance, poised between the extremes of left, right, forward, and back. But, above all, we keep happy, brimming with the benefits of a fully fledged philosophy. On a bike we experience the magical joy of curiosity; the exhilaration of a mind in free flow; the warm glow of belonging and contributing to a community; and the awe inspired by nature's wildness, or humanity at its most profound. On a bike we discover what Einstein knew all along—that whatever life throws at us, everything is alright.

INDEX

FURTHER READING & RESOURCES

Beaumont, M., *The Man Who Cycled the World* (Bantam Press, London, 2009)

Cavill, N. and Davis, A., *Cycling and Health: What's the Evidence?* (2007)
(http://www.ecf.com/wp-content/uploads/2011/10/Cycling-and-health-Whats-the-evidence.pdf)

Crawford, M., *The Case for Working with Your Hands: Or Why Office Work is Bad for Us and Fixing Things Feels Good* (Viking, London, 2009)

Cycle Lifestyle magazine: all issues available for free download at www.cyclelifestyle.co.uk

Heaversedge, J. and Halliwell, E., *The Mindful Manifesto: How Doing Less and Noticing More Can Help us Thrive in a Stressed-out World* (Hay House, London, 2010)

Herlihy, D.V., *Bicycle: The History* (Yale University Press, New Haven, 2004)

Isaacson, W., *Einstein: His Life and Universe* (Simon & Schuster, London, 2007)

Layard, R., *Happiness: Lessons from a New Science* (Penguin, London, 2005)

Parsons, P., *3-Minute Einstein: Digesting his Life, Theories, and Influence in 3-Minute Morsels* (Metro Books, New York, 2011)

Penn, R., *It's All About the Bike: The Pursuit of Happiness on Two Wheels* (Particular Books, London, 2010)

Putnam, R., *Bowling Alone: The Collapse and Revival of American Community* (Simon & Schuster, New York, 2000)

Wilkinson, R. and Pickett, K., *The Spirit Level: Why More Equal Societies Almost Always Do Better* (Allen Lane, London, 2009)

Wright, R., *Nonzero: History, Evolution & Human Cooperation* (Abacus, London, 2001)